AN INTRODUCTION TO
HADITH

AYHAN TEKİNEŞ

AN INTRODUCTION TO
HADITH

AYHAN TEKİNEŞ

TUGHRA
BOOKS

New Jersey

Originally published in Turkish as *Bilgi Kaynağı Olarak Hadis* in 2005

18 17 16 15   1 2 3 4

Published by Tughra Books
345 Clifton Ave., Clifton,
NJ, 07011, USA

www.tughrabooks.com

Library of Congress Cataloging-in-Publication Data

Tekines, Ayhan, 1964-
[Bilgi kaynagi olarak hadis. English]
An introduction to hadith / Ayhan Tekines.
pages cm
ISBN 978-1-59784-317-1 (alk. paper)
1. Hadith. I. Title.
BP135.T4313 2014
297.1'25161--dc23
2014036467

ISBN: 978-1-59784-317-1

Printed by
Çağlayan A.Ş., Izmir - Turkey

CONTENTS

UNIT FIVE
INTENTION, SINCERITY

UNIT SIX
IMAN, ISLAM, *IHSAN*

UNIT SEVEN
REPENTANCE, SEEKING FORGIVENESS

UNIT EIGHT
PATIENCE

UNIT NINE
MUI IASABA – MURAQABA (SELF-CRITICISM AND SELF-SUPERVISION)

UNIT TEN
AVOIDING INNOVATION

An Introduction to Hadith

INTRODUCTION

In this work, the Hadith studies and its lexicon have been examined from a historical and literary perspective. Terminology is of paramount importance in the Hadith studies, with there being hundreds of terms therein. Those terms that are important in understanding such a discipline have been identified and defined in this book.

The elucidation of these terms alone is not sufficient, however, in acquiring a grasp of the Hadith studies. Thus, these have been examined together with their historical development. Sheer description of the history of Hadith studies has not been pursued in explaining the significant phases of the history of Hadith; instead, its nomenclature has been considered alongside its history.

One of the most important elements in the Hadith studies is the literature, for the books of Hadith of the first Islamic century constitute the primary sources of the religion of Islam. Knowledge of these primary sources and an awareness of exactly how we are to benefit from these are indispensable. Accordingly, seminal texts on the hadiths are introduced in this work and information pertaining to their key aspects provided. In view of an introduction to the various works of hadith playing a pivotal role in gaining an understanding of the specific topic at hand, a brief summary is provided at the end of each topic.

The key topics of the Hadith studies are explained in general terms and the lucid clarification of each topic aimed at, without there being much reference to controversy and difference of opinion. What has been sought, more so, is a concise demonstration of the functioning of the knowledge system itself.

In studies with matters pertaining to the history of Hadith as their subject matter, it becomes evident that they, more often than not, deal at length with exceptional cases that have no direct bearing on the essence of the topic at hand and, as such, serve to distract and confuse more than anything. Essential in every discipline, first and foremost, is an explanation of the main guidelines and essentials, with exceptional cases and circumstances being investigated only by those with necessary expertise. Otherwise, the issues expounded are fated to remain in the shadow of unorthodox and dissident views.

Works, as much as individuals, are of importance in epistemology. Consequently, information relating to the founders of the Hadith studies, the Companions of the noble Prophet, is provided in addition to information regarding their successors and later hadith scholars.

Terminology, references, and information concerning personalities and methodology are presented in a comprehensible fashion. Nonetheless, it is still possible to encounter certain difficulties in understanding the topic at hand. Questions with regard to the various topics are offered at the end of each unit, in view of overcoming these difficulties. It is envisaged that further research into the answers to these questions, and instructors' more extensive responses to these, will facilitate greater understanding.

UNIT ONE

THE HADITH STUDIES
AND THE SUNNAH

MEANING OF "HADITH"

The Arabic word *hadith* denotes "news" or "tidings" and "a word," with the plural form being *ahadith*. In ancient Arabic, the term was employed to express important news and words that are esteemed. The Arabs used to refer to the news of their famous and important days in pre-Islamic Arabia as *ahadith* and would describe those expressions that had become idioms as *sara hadithan* or *sara uhdutha*, meaning "it has become a *hadith*," or "it has become a thing, or matter, that is called of, told, or narrated, and transmitted". The word *hadith* has been employed in the Qur'an to mean a special discourse. In the Qur'anic verses, "*...let them produce a discourse like it*," (at-Tur 52:34) and "*Allah sends down in parts the best of the words...*," (az-Zumar 39:23) *hadith* denotes a special word, or sign. The term also comes to mean "news" or "tidings." The word is used in the verse, "*Has the report of Moses come to you?*" (Ta-Ha 20:9) refers to news.

Just as the word hadith is mentioned in the Qur'an, it is also referred to in the words of Allah's Messenger, upon him be peace and blessings. The Prophet's Companion Abu Hurayra, one of those most avid to acquire knowledge from him, once came to him and inquired about the person who will be happiest with his intercession on the Day of Judgment. The Messenger of Allah, peace and blessings be upon him, said, "Abu Hurayra, I thought that none would ask about this *hadith* (this word) before you since I know your eagerness for *hadith* [i.e. learning]." The Messenger's using the word *hadith* in reference to his own words constituted a model for his Companions. Thereafter, his words were referred to as *hadith* and the discipline constituting the study of these *hadith*s was called *Ilm al-Hadith*, or the Hadith Studies.

The Hadith Studies has also been called *Usul al-Hadith*, or the methodology of Hadith criticism. Hadith scholars have determined a set of rules for the preservation of the Prophet's words and the communications of his Companions describing him, and to enable their transfer to succeeding generations without alteration; as such, they have put forth a specific methodology. The discipline wherein these methods are expounded has been referred to as the "science of Hadith methodology." With the substance of its subject matter flourishing over time, all of its various branches have virtually each become separate disciplines unto themselves. Independent studies have been conducted in relation to each of these disciplines. The entirety of all these disciplines has together been referred to as the "Hadith Sciences" *(Ulum al-Hadith)*.

When reference was made to knowledge in the first Islamic century, the Hadith Sciences were specifically implied, by virtue of their significance. When many separate disciplines arose examining the hadith from myriad perspectives, all of these were collectively referred to as *Ulum al-Hadith*. Author of one of the first works in the field of the Hadith Sciences, Hakim al-Nisaburi (d. 1014 CE), titled his book *Ma'rifat Ulum al-Hadith*. Ibn al-Salah (d. 1245 CE) penned the most important work examining the Hadith Sciences, entitled *Ulum al-Hadith*. Topics expounded in these works such as *sahih hadith* and *hasan hadith*s have each been accepted as separate disciplines, for there are a great number of sub-branches and literature which have accumulated under each.

SCOPE OF THE TERM HADITH

In the same way that the words and sayings of Allah's Messenger, peace and blessings be upon him, are referred to as hadith, the words of the Companions regarding an incident involving him or reporting one of his actions has also come to be known as hadith. The Prophet's words, his actions, and decisions as well as the practices that he approved of, allowed or condoned, and reports pertaining to his disposition and character have also been included in this category.

For instance, the Messenger of Allah, peace and blessings be upon him, has said, "The Prayer performed without the prescribed ablution is not accepted."[1] This saying is a Tradition that Abdullah ibn Umar, may Allah be pleased with him, heard from the noble Prophet and narrated. Ali's narration that "The Prophet performed ablution three times (for each limb),"[2] is again a hadith attributed to the Messenger of Allah, peace and blessings be upon him, for it is Ali's report indicating the noble Prophet's behavior.

THE MEANING OF SUNNAH

The word Sunnah, denoting such things as the visible part of the face, appearance, path, character and nature, has acquired a particular meaning in the Islamic scholarly tradition and has been used to refer to the path pursued by the Prophet in his life and in his actions. The term encompasses the willful actions or deeds of Allah's Messenger, peace and blessings be upon him; similarly, it also includes his morality, character and humanity. He is the greatest example for humanity, in his every aspect and manner. There are models of behavior for human beings in his every deliberate and unintentional action.

Alongside the widely accepted literal meaning of the word Sunnah—"a way," "road" or "path"—is its being used to refer to a thing's distinctive characteristics. The words, actions and behavior of the Prophet have become a path followed by human beings and the ostensible, pronounced characteristics of the religion have become known through the Sunnah.

The Sunnah are the words, practices and approvals—collectively—of Allah's Messenger, peace and blessings be upon him, while the hadiths are the duly reported narrations that convey these words, actions, and approvals (*taqrir*). The Sunnah has been identified and recorded by means of the hadith. The Sunnah can only be known for certain in our day through the hadith. In other words, the Sunnah is known via the narrations of hadith scholars. Such being the case, in periods succeeding the Age of Happiness, the words Sunnah and hadith have more often than not been used interchangeably.

---

[1] *Sunan at-Tirmidhi*, Tahara, 1

[2] *Sunan at-Tirmidhi*, Tahara, 34

The word having a meaning opposite to the term Sunnah is *bid'a*, meaning something introduced later or an innovation contrary to religion. Over time, Sunnah also assumed sociological signification, with those dedicated to the way of the Prophet being known as *ahl al-Sunnah* (those devoted to the Sunnah) and opponents being called *ahl al-bid'a* (people of innovation in religion).

SCOPE OF SUNNAH

The word Sunnah has acquired different meanings across different disciplines. Every discipline has employed the term with a meaning suitable to its own particular methodology. Jurists have used Sunnah as the antithesis of *bid'a* as well as those narrations which serve as the source of legal rulings. According to them, hadith and Sunnah are in this sense synonymous. In books of Islamic jurisprudence, however, Sunnah is used to mean those religious commandments which are not religiously obligatory or necessary for human beings.

In Islamic legal theory, or methodology of *fiqh*, Sunnah represents the communications of the Prophet, outside the Qur'an, conducive to functioning as demonstrative evidence. Moreover, not being restricted to its evidential nature, Sunnah has also been defined as everything, other than the Qur'an, issuing from Allah's Messenger, peace and blessings be upon him.[3]

The practice of the Companions has also been called Sunnah, for their practice could well be conveying a Prophetic practice that has not reached us in the form of a hadith.[4] For this reason, the words and sayings of the Companions have been related by scholars of hadith (*muhaddithin*) along with their list of transmitters, like the hadith. The Companions' devotion to the Sunnah led them to either seeking a particular practice of the Prophet in their every act, or to determining their way via independent reasoning (*ijtihad*) in accord with the Sunnah. Moreover, Allah's Messenger, peace

---

[3] Shatibi, *Al-Muwafaqat*, 4:1; M. Fethullah Gülen, *Muhammad: The Messenger of God*, 316

[4] Shatibi, *Al-Muwafaqat*, 4:2

and blessings be upon him, himself enjoined his community to follow the Four Rightly-Guided Caliphs, may Allah be pleased with them, who succeeded him: "Hold fast to my Sunnah and the Sunnah of the Rightly-Guided Caliphs."[5]

HADITH *QUDSI*

Among the revelations communicated to the noble Prophet, the words of which cannot be recited in worship, are the words ascribed to Allah. The Prophet conveyed these words from his Lord, to the people. These Traditions are referred to as *Hadith Qudsi* or Divine Hadith. For instance, Allah's Messenger, peace and blessings be upon him, stated that Allah said, "My mercy prevails over My wrath."[6] These words are those belonging to Allah verbatim. However, as this statement was not revealed to the Prophet as part of the Qur'an, it is not a Qur'anic verse. Due to its wording not being communicated through revelation, it is also not of a miraculous nature with respect to its wording. As a result, it cannot be recited in place of the Qur'an during the Prescribed Prayer.

The words narrated by Allah's Messenger, peace and blessings be upon him, as the words of Allah are juristically subject to the rules which apply to hadith. By means of adding His words among those of His Messenger, Allah the Almighty demonstrates the value and regard He places upon him and his Sunnah.

IMPORTANCE OF ADHERENCE
TO THE SUNNAH

Those who best know the Sunnah's importance are the Companions. They preferred adherence to the Sunnah to everything else. When Abu Bakr, may Allah be pleased with him, was appointed caliph, the Prophet's daughter Fatima went to him and requested her share in the Prophet's inheri-

---

[5]   *Sunan at-Tirmidhi*, Ilm, 16
[6]   *Sahih al-Bukhari*, Tawhid, 15

tance. Despite his loving the Prophet's relatives more than his own, he reminded Fatima of something he had heard from Allah's Messenger, peace and blessings be upon him. He had heard something from the noble Messenger, which Fatima had not: "We, the community of the Prophets, do not bequeath anything. Whatever we leave is charity."[7] He thus declined Fatima's request. Such was his faithfulness to the Sunnah that it had overcome even his own sentiment.

The Companions preferred the Sunnah to their own views and opinions. If there was a hadith in relation to a particular matter, they immediately followed it, and when they were made aware of a hadith that they had hitherto not known, they would instantly abandon their own views and adhere to that hadith. During his caliphate, Umar ibn al-Khattab, may Allah be pleased with him, had embarked on an expedition to Syria for the purpose of inspecting the army. When he heard that pestilence had broken out in Amwas, he was undecided as to whether or not he should return to Medina. Abdu'r-Rahman ibn Awf, may Allah be pleased with him, said to him: "I heard the Messenger say: 'If you hear that pestilence has broken out in a place, do not enter it. If you are in such a place already, do not leave it.'" Upon hearing these words, Umar returned without hesitation.[8]

Known for his sagacity and knowledge, Ali, may Allah be pleased with him, said in reference to wiping over indoor boots during the ritual ablution: "If the religion were based on opinion, it would be more important to wipe the under part of the shoe than the upper but I have seen the Messenger of Allah, peace and blessings be upon him, wiping over the upper part of his shoes."[9] With these words, he has drawn attention to the transcendental nature of religion and has expressed the importance of adherence to the Sunnah.

The Prophets are exempted by Allah from all kinds of sin and wrongdoing. Allah has sent down upon them His blessing and mercy and has

---

[7] *Sahih al-Bukhari*, Khums, 1

[8] *Sahih al-Bukhari*, Tibb, 29

[9] *Sunan Abu Dawud*, Tahara, 63

commanded the believers to entreat Him for the Prophets and demonstrate their attachment to them with the following Qur'anic verse:

> Surely Allah and His angels bless the Prophet (He always treats him with His special mercy, with the angels praying to Him to grant him the highest station of praise with Him, and for the decisive victory of his Religion). O you who believe, invoke the blessings of Allah on him, and pray to Allah to bestow His peace on him, greeting him with the best greeting. (Love and follow him with utmost sincerity and faithfulness, and give yourselves to his way with perfect submission). (al-Ahzab 33:56)

Deeming the fulfillment of the injunction in this verse a religious obligation, Muslim scholars have asserted that saying "peace be upon him" (*alayhis-salam*) when the names of Prophets are mentioned and "upon him be peace and blessings" (*sallallahu alayhi wa sallam*) at the mention of Prophet Muhammad's name, upon him be peace and blessings, is indispensable.

Invoking the peace and blessings of Allah upon Allah's Messenger at the first mention of his name is necessary (*wajib*), while recommended and rewarded (*mustahab*) at repeat mentions. Furthermore, such expressions of praise and devotion as "noble Messenger" and "most illustrious Prophet", in prefix to his name, at each and every invocation is demonstration of our reverence and respect to him.

EVALUATION

1. Define the term "hadith."
2. Which words are referred to as "hadith?"
3. Define the term Sunnah.
4. In what senses has the term Sunnah been used?
5. How must the Sunnah's being revelation-based be understood?
6. In which Qur'anic verses is the word *hikma* (wisdom) used to mean Sunnah?
7. What are the characteristics differentiating Hadith *Qudsi* from other hadith?

UNIT TWO

THE *SAHABA* AND THE *TABI'UN*

DEFINITION OF *SAHABA*

The Companions of the noble Messenger are referred to as *Sahabi* (pl. *Sahaba* or *Ashab*), denoting 'companion, associate, comrade, fellow, friend, or fellow-traveler' in Arabic. Those believers who saw and heard the noble Messenger at least once, and who died as Muslims have been referred to as *Sahabi*.

VIRTUES OF THE *SAHABA*

There are many verses in the Qur'an that speak of the virtue of the Prophet's Companions. It is said of them, *"Allah was assuredly well-pleased with the believers when they swore allegiance to you under the tree"* (al-Fath 48:18). Due to Allah's saying of them, "Allah is well-pleased with them," it has become common to say, "May Allah be well pleased with them," when one of their names are mentioned.

Allah has revealed that the Companions are sincere, straightforward and trustworthy, and indeed prosperous;[10] stating, *"You are the best community ever brought forth for (the good of) humankind,"* (Al Imran 3:110) He has praised them in the greatest possible way. Allah's Messenger, peace and blessings be upon him, has echoed the same notion in his hadith stating, "The best of people are my generation and then those who follow them and then those who follow them."[11]

Due to the Qur'an and Sunnah's confirming the righteousness and morality Companions without any differentiation between them and its attesting to their piety and fairness, all the Companions have been accepted as righteous. Implied in the term "righteous" (*adil*) is the reliability of their testimony, their truthfulness, faithfulness, piety, trustworthiness and steadfast-

---

[10]   Al-Hashr 59:8–9
[11]   *Sahih al-Bukhari*, Fada'il al-Ashab, 1

ness. The *Ahl al-Sunnah* scholars have unanimously accepted all the Companions to be righteous. On account of this, speaking ill of or insulting any of the Companions has been considered as one of the greatest of sins. The most illustrious Prophet has stated: "Do not curse my Companions! Do not curse my Companions! I swear by Him in Whose hand my life is that, even if one among you had as much gold as Mount Uhud and spent it in the way of Allah, this would not be equal in reward to a few handfuls of them or even to half of that."[12]

The Companions have been grouped into various categories among them, based on their level of virtue. The Meccan Companions have been referred to as the Emigrants (*Muhajirun*), while the Medinan natives have been called the Helpers (*Ansar*). They have been ranked in accordance with their participation in such important events as the Battle of Badr and the oath of allegiance. The Prophet's household (*Ahl al-Bayt*), children, wives and relatives hold a distinct position and esteem. The Messenger of Allah, peace and blessings be upon him, said that his daughter, "Fatima is the mistress of the women of Paradise," and in another hadith, stated, "Fatima is part of me. Whoever makes her angry, makes me angry."[13] He also revealed that Archangel Jabrail gave his greetings to his wife Aisha, may Allah be pleased with her, and said in one hadith, "Do not injure me regarding Aisha."[14]

The most virtuous of the Companions are the four Rightly-Guided Caliphs, respectively. One of the most well-known gradations is the ten Companions who were promised Paradise while still alive (*Ashara al-Mubashshara*). They are Abu Bakr (d. 634 CE), Umar (d. 644 CE), Uthman (d. 655 CE), Ali (d. 660 CE), Abdu'r-Rahman ibn Awf (d. 652 CE), Abu Ubayda ibn al-Jarrah (d. 639 CE), Talha ibn Ubaydullah (d. 656 CE), Zubayr ibn al-Awwam (d. 656 CE), Said ibn Zayd ibn Amr (d. 671 CE), and Sa'd ibn Abi Waqqas (d. 675 CE), may Allah be well pleased with all of them.

THE *TABI'UN*

---

[12] *Sahih Muslim*, Fada'il al-Sahaba, 221
[13] *Sahih al-Bukhari*, Fada'il al-Ashab, 29
[14] *Sahih al-Bukhari*, Fada'il al-Ashab, 30

Those succeeding the Companions and following in their footsteps have been referred to as *Tabi'i* (pl. *Tabi'un*), being a person who met with one of the Companions and spent time in their company. Allah declares that He is well pleased with those who follow in the footsteps of the Companions:

وَالسَّابِقُونَ الْأَوَّلُونَ مِنَ الْمُهَاجِرِينَ وَالْأَنْصَارِ وَالَّذِينَ اتَّبَعُوهُمْ بِاحْسَانٍ رَضِيَ اللهُ عَنْهُمْ وَرَضُوا عَنْهُ وَأَعَدَّ لَهُمْ جَنَّاتٍ تَجْرِى تَحْتَهَا الْأَنْهَارُ خَالِدِينَ فِيهَا أَبَداً ذَلِكَ الْفَوْزُ الْعَظِيمُ

The first and foremost (to embrace Islam and excel others in virtue) among the Emigrants and the Helpers, and those who follow them in devotion to doing good, aware that Allah is seeing them—Allah is well-pleased with them, and they are well-pleased with Him, and He has prepared for them Gardens throughout which rivers flow, therein to abide forever. That is the supreme triumph. (at-Tawbah 9:100)

Allah's Messenger, peace and blessings be upon him, states that the best generation after his Companions is the one succeeding them.

The generation of the *Tabi'un* is of utmost importance with respect to the history of Islamic religious studies. The greatest Muslim scholars lived in this generation and the principles of the Islamic studies determined by them. The following seven Medinan scholars known as the *Seven Jurists of Medina* (*Fuqaha al-Medina as-Sab'a*), have especial importance in the Hadith Sciences: Said ibn al-Mussayyib (d. 723 CE), Qasim ibn Muhammad (d. 723 CE), Urwa ibn Zubayr (d. 713 CE), Kharija ibn Zayd ibn Thabit (d. 718 CE), Abu Salama ibn Abdu'r-Rahman ibn Awf (d. 722 CE), Ubayd Allah ibn Utba ibn Mas'ud (d. 717 CE), and Sulayman ibn Yasar (d. 722 CE). Relatives of the Companions and raised among them, these *Tabi'un* scholars became known through the consultations they held among themselves in resolving issues. With strong command of the Qur'an and Sunnah in terms of both transmission (*riwaya*) and critical perception or cognition (*diraya*), *Tabi'un* scholars established the Islamic studies on strong intellectual grounds.

EVALUATION

1. Who is known as a Companion?
2. Who are the *mukthirun* Companions?
3. Which Companions narrate *mursal* hadith?
4. Who is referred to as *mukhadram*?
5. Who is known as the *Tabi'un*?

UNIT THREE

SAHIH AND *HASAN* HADITH

DEFINITION OF *SAHIH* HADITH

From the moment the hadith were first recorded onwards, they were meticulously protected with even the slightest errors not being overlooked, but identified. Certain essentials have been established in view of preserving the Prophetic Traditions and preventing transmission-based errors. Traditions consonant with these essentials and criteria have been regarded as acceptable, or *maqbul*, while those that are not have been rejected. The acceptable hadiths have been likened to a fit and healthy human being and labeled sound (*sahih*), while the others have been labeled defective (*saqim*) or faulty (*mu'allal*).

The first and most fundamental prerequisite for a hadith to be classified as sound is the integrity and trustworthiness of its narrator. Due to there being not even the slightest doubt with regard to the character of the Companions, all of them have been accepted to bear the characteristic of truth and righteousness. The second precondition is that the narrator possesses strong intellectual capacity or academic competence. A very strong memory and reliability in written documentation, in the event that their transmission is in written form, as well as above average intelligence are the most important qualities sought in the narrator.

With the chain of narrators lengthening over time, the connection between mentor and student being known gained increasing importance. A strong and reliable mentor-student relationship came to be accepted as one of the prerequisites of a sound hadith. Those wanting to learn or record hadith from a particular mentor, accepted as a basis recording from their most reliable students who spent the longest time with them. The aim, in so doing, is to reduce any student error and eliminate the possibility of misattribution.

The possibility for error exists in narrations with reliable narrators and a sound mentor-student connection also. In view of eliminating such possibilities of error as misapprehension and omission, the hadith narrated by various students of the same mentor have been compared and cross-checked for soundness. In this way, an attempt has been made to identify errors that can arise in respect to its chain of narrators (*isnad*).

The necessary conditions of sound Traditions became evident as a result of the check and control mechanism which developed in parallel with the growing chain of narrators and increasing number of narrations. Accordingly: 1) The narrator must be righteous, 2) possess a very strong memory; 3) the mentor-student connection must be sound; 4) the narration must not be anomalous (*shadh*) or 5) faulty (*mu'allal*).

Mu'allal hadiths are those, which although outwardly reliable and sound, reveal a hidden flaw. As is evident, a Tradition's possessing the qualities of authenticity or soundness with respect to form and its transmission by reliable narrators has not been deemed sufficient. The need for its verification by specialist hadith scholars, or Traditionists, has also been emphasized.

Traditionists have never been bound by form and have not shown absolute submission to authority. They have not neglected research and verification. To that end, they have examined the narrations of the most reliable hadith scholars and have attached even greater importance to investigating their shortcomings, for it is much more difficult to pick up on the errors of a reliable narrator.

Alongside the small number of hadith texts, or *matn*, each different narration emerging as a result of change in narrators in the chain of transmission has been regarded as a separate hadith. For instance, in the event of a Tradition narrated by a single Companion being transmitted by two of his students, these have been accepted as two separate Traditions and when those two students have each had five students, they have been regarded as ten separate hadith. In this way, the number of narrations multiplied along with the increasing number of students and by the third Islamic century, approximately one million narrations had become distributed among the students of the Hadith Sciences. Traditionists have made selections from among these narrations within the framework of certain criteria.

IMAM BUKHARI'S *SAHIH*

Due to the fact that weak Traditions have been accepted as evidence historically and in matters pertaining to the virtue of certain personalities and places, as well as in legal issues lacking rulings, they have been narrated and even recorded in compilations by hadith scholars. In this period, "fair" or *hasan* hadith were also evaluated in the category of weak hadith. On account of such issues as the criticism leveled at Traditionists for narrating weak hadith and the difficulty for those other than the hadith scholars to benefit from books of hadith, Traditionist Ishaq ibn Rahuya (d. 852 CE) referred to—in an assembly where his student Bukhari was also present—the need for a compilation containing only the rigorously authenticated (*sahih*) hadith.

Beginning his work upon this advice, Imam Bukhari (d. 870 CE) selected 1,563 hadiths from among the 600,000 that he had collected until that point, to produce his work *Al-Jami' as-sahih*. The full title of the work is *Al-Jami al-Musnad as-Sahih al-Mukhtasar min Umur Rasulullah wa Sunanihi wa Ayyamihi* (The Abridged Authentic Compilation of the Affairs of the Messenger of Allah, his Sunnah and Campaigns). The term *mukhtasar* in the title, denoting "concise," serves to illustrate that he did not aim to compile all authentic Traditions. As a matter of fact, after Bukhari, a great many authors produced works compiling *sahih* hadith; however, Bukhari's collection has always been accepted as the most reliable with respect to both its being the first of its kind and due to his rigorous application of the *sahih* hadith criteria. The reliability of his narrations pertains to his work in the general sense. A particular narration in another hadith compilation may be sounder than the one in Bukhari and it is possible to find sounder narration than one cited in Bukhari.

Later scholars of hadith conducted various studies on Imam Bukhari's work, investigating his narrators one by one, discovering differing chains of transmission for the narrations therein, and carrying out independent studies of its diverse characteristics. Imam Bukhari's work left researchers in awe of him and has been regarded as the most reputable book of hadith.

Bukhari recorded narrations from approximately one thousand mentors, but included the narrations of only 293 of his mentors in his *Sahih*. The shortest chain of transmission in Bukhari's *Sahih* contains three narrators. There are twenty-two such hadith in the work, with the number of narrators for each *isnad* throughout varying between three and six. Bukhari has documented the narrations of the most select narrators at each level or category. He has included a total 1,597 narrators, 208 of them Companions.

Bukhari's work is divided into ninety-seven chapters (*kutub*, sing. *kitab*) and subdivided into 3,730 subchapters (*abwab*, sing. *bab*). The use of the term *jami* (compilation) in the title suggests that the work brings together Prophetic Traditions covering a complete range of topics. After beginning with a hadith on the matter or intention, it proceeds with a section explaining the beginning of revelation, and passes on to legal issues after expounding matters of belief and knowledge. Chapters concerning history and related topics begin with the creation of the universe and continue with sections explaining the history of previous Prophets and the military expeditions (*maghazi*) of Allah's Messenger, peace and blessings be upon him. Including an extensive treatment on the Qur'anic commentary (*tafsir*), the work's subchapters have been enriched with explanatory notes taken from various works of commentary up until his day.

Bukhari has given room to his own opinions and those of other writers in only the subheadings. He has also included Qur'anic verses in some subheadings, citing these in particular in the subheadings of the last chapter, the Book of *Tawhid*. In his work, Imam Bukhari has also collected hadith encompassing all aspects of life such as dreams, medicine, illnesses, and good character.

Bukhari has aimed not only to compile the hadith themselves, but to also facilitate rulings to be obtained from them and to allow the hadith to serve as a guide in every facet of life. For this reason, he has scattered the hadith under a great many subheadings, even sometimes repeating a single hadith under the relevant six or seven subheadings. While there are a total of 7,275 hadiths, this number is reduced to 2,791 upon a removal of all duplicates. By means of including a different chain of transmission (*isnad*, sing. *sanad*) or content or text (*matn*) at each repetition of the hadith, he avoids the possibility of their being rendered meaningless. Sometimes, for the purpose of abridgement, he has not cited the chain of narrators for the repeated hadith. Placing these hadith in the subheadings, he has been able to include a great number of hadith in his work without making it any greater in volume.

IMAM MUSLIM'S *SAHIH*

Muslim ibn Hajjaj al-Qushayri's (d. 874 CE) *Al-Jami as-Sahih* is one of the most important of hadith canons. Muslim is the student of prominent scholars such as Ahmad ibn Hanbal and Imam Bukhari. In his work, he has included 7,563 hadiths from among 300,000, separating these into chapters but not entitling these. There are fifty-four main chapters ("Books") in the book. He has not repeated the hadith under separate subheadings, but has placed differing narrations of the same hadith consecutively in the same section. The majority of the hadith in the work are those included in Bukhari. A hadith mentioned in the collections of both Bukhari and Muslim is referred to as *muttafaqun alayh* (agreed upon). There are 820 hadiths in Muslim that are not included in Bukhari's compilation.

SAHIHAYN

The works of Bukhari and Muslim are known as the *Sahihayn* (the two *sahih*). The hadith agreed upon by both are referred to as *muttafaqun alayh* and have been regarded as the soundest hadith.

Muslim has not adopted the approach of transmission by meaning, summarization and a hadith's being narrated under different headings. He has placed primary importance on preserving the original words of the hadith and transmission verbatim. Hence, when hadith agreed upon by both Bukhari and Muslim are transmitted, the latter's text is generally preferred. The legal dimension takes precedence in Bukhari's text, while adherence to the methodology of hadith transmission holds sway in Muslim.

MAQBUL HADITH

Maqbul, or acceptable hadiths have been divided into two parts: sound (*sahih*) and fair (*hasan*). The term 'fair' hadith has been used to illustrate the differentiation in degree between different hadith in the absence of any flaw affecting the soundness of a hadith in terms of its transmission. As the Arabic word *hasan* denotes 'beautiful' and 'pleasant', it was employed by second century scholars in their studies of hadith to also signify sound hadith, in line with is literal meaning. From the third Islamic century onwards, however, it became a specialized term representing acceptable hadith that could not be classified as *sahih*.

In addition to the terms *sahih* and *hasan*, the words *jayyid*, meaning good and amiable, *thabit*, and *salih* have been used in reference to acceptable (*maqbul*) hadith.

DEFINITION OF *HASAN* HADITH

The first individual to define the term *hasan* hadith was Abu Isa Muhammad ibn Isa at-Tirmidhi (d. 892 CE). Imam Tirmidhi defined hadith whose narrators were not alleged to have lied, that were not opposed to other authenticated hadith and which had a second supporting narration, as *hasan*. Tirmidhi kept the scope of the meaning of *hasan* hadith quite broad and accepted weak hadith that were corroborated with a second chain of transmission as fair. Referred to in this definition are narrations that are not themselves directly fair, but which achieve such a status through a second supporting chain of narration. Consequently, Tirmidhi's definition expresses those hadith that are *hasan li-ghayrihi*, or *hasan* due to other narrations.

As for hadith that are *hasan li-dhatihi*, or *hasan* in itself, they have been defined differently. Accordingly, *hasan* hadith bear all the characteristics of sound hadith, but contain a shortcoming with respect to the documentation of one of its narrators. Such deficiencies include those such as any weakness in the narrator's memory or an occasional lapse. However, it is essential that these narrators be renowned for hadith narration and be reliable and righteous. The narrations of those narrators who carry these characteristics and which do not contradict those of reliable narrators and have no

other defect with respect to transmission, have been regarded as fair.

EVALUATION

1. Define *sahih* hadith.

2. Explain the accumulation of *sahih* hadith.

3. What are the distinctive characteristics of Bukhari's *Sahih*?

4. What are the distinctive characteristics of Muslim's *Sahih*?

5. What are the differences in the works of Bukhari and Muslim?

6. Explain *maqbul* hadith.

7. Define *hasan* hadith.

8. What does *i'tibar* in the Hadith Sciences refer to?

9. What is *hasan li-ghayrihi*?

UNIT FOUR

WEAK HADITH AND HADITH

FABRICATION

WEAK HADITH DEFINED

H adith that are not acceptable with regard to the criteria concerning their reliability have been regarded as rejected, or *mardud*. Such hadiths have also been referred to with the word *saqim* (unsound or infirm) used as the opposite of *sahih*. Weak hadiths are those which do not possess at least one of the five determined preconditions for the soundness of hadith. Some scholars have asserted that there are forty-two different kinds of weak hadith.

The weakness or unsoundness of hadith stems from the inadequacy of the narrator in terms of righteousness and academic competence (*zabt*). However, there needs to be explicit proof demonstrating the narrator's shortcoming with regard to piety or scholarly competence. This proof is comprised of defects in the narrations they transmit. On account of this, hadith scholars have preferred assessments putting forth errors in narration to weakness in the narrator, in their hadith critique.

TYPES OF WEAK HADITH

The most well-known of weak (*da'if*) hadiths have been named in accordance with their various defects in transmission. Hadith with a continuity of transmission, or chain of narration, are referred to as *muttasil*. The chain of *sahih* hadiths are *muttasil*, or continuous. Discontinuity in the chain of narration is a flaw affecting the soundness of hadith; however, as all discontinuities in transmission do not constitute a cause for weakness to the same degree, each of them has been referred to with different names. A chain of transmission with the Companion's name missing is called *mursal*, one with two or more consecutive narrators missing is called *mu'dal*, a suspended chain with the names of one or more mentors omitted by the author is referred to as *mu'allaq*, and *munqati* is the general term used to refer to a broken chain where at least one narrator is missing.

Another kind of weak hadith is that which is anomalous or *shadhdh*. The hadith in which a hadith transmitter who is accepted to be reliable (*thiqa*) contradicts a more reliable transmitter or other transmitters, is referred to as an anomalous hadith. This contradiction can pertain to both the chain and the actual text of the hadith.

In cases where opposition to a reliable narrator is on the part of a weak narrator, this hadith is called *munkar*, or singular and suspect. Due to the fact that *munkar* constitute a weak transmitter's opposition to a reliable hadith transmitter, they possess two significant defects. Therefore, these have been regarded as being among the weakest types of hadith. There have also been those who have deemed narrations that are unfamiliar to hadith scholars as *munkar* purely due to their being unknown. However, it has become common to term such hadith as singular or "strange" (*gharib*) hadith, possessing only one transmitter at some stage of the chain.

Such singular hadiths have not been accepted as one of the types of weak hadith in the absolute sense, but there are many weak hadith among them. This is because there are no subsequent traditions supporting them. Consequently, hadith scholars have attached importance to examining singular hadith and have penned independent works in this regard. For instance, Bazar's *Musnad* and Tabarani's *Al-Mujam al-Awsat* are compilations of singular hadith and investigations of their soundness.

Narrations where the hadith transmitter has rearranged a word or sentence in the text of the hadith or where the names of some of the transmitters of the chain of transmission are altered, are called inverted or transposed (*maqlub*) hadith.

RULING PERTAINING TO WEAK HADITH

All weak hadiths are not equal in degree. Narrations have been classified in accordance with the situation of the transmitters and their opposition to or contradiction with other hadith transmitters. Hadiths have been graded by means of comparisons between narrations, from the most reliable to the weakest.

Although sound and fair hadith constitute evidence in every matter, weak hadiths have only been accepted as proof in certain subject areas. Due to the likelihood of their being the Prophet's words, weak hadiths have been considered in the absence of sound hadith. Weak hadiths have been accepted in such issues as the praise, criticism or encouragement of a matter established in sound hadith. In addition, they have been appropriated as a supporting and buttressing element. However, there are certain types of weak hadith that have been completely abandoned. Such narrations are referred to as disregarded (*matruk*) narrations and they have not been considered under any circumstances.

The following three conditions are necessary for a weak hadith to be accepted: 1) The transmitted hadith must not be very weak; 2) It must not contradict the Qur'an and Sunnah; and 3) It must be based on a principle established in the Qur'an and the Sunnah. As is evident, a weak hadith has not been accepted as evidence with regard to a non-existent judgment or ruling. However, it has been used for the purposes of encouragement, caution or recommendation, consonant with the essence of the religion, in existing matters that have already been firmly demonstrated.

RELIGIOUS RULING CONCERNING LYING

Just as there were those individuals in the Prophet's lifetime who claimed to be prophets and claimed to have received revelation, there were also those who tried to ascribe words to the Prophet that he did not utter. In the face of such an event, Allah's Messenger, peace and blessings be upon him, stated: "Those who intentionally lie against me should prepare their abode in the

Fire."[15] Again in another hadith, the Prophet declared that one who trans-mits a lie is also considered to have lied: "It is sufficient lying for a man to repeat that he hears."[16]

In Islam, lying (*kidhb*) has virtually been equated with unbelief. In the Qur'an, the term 'denial' has been used in reference to rejecting Allah and religion. In contrast, *sidq* denotes believing and affirming the truth of religion. On account of this, the Companions conceived of falsehood and truth as two diametrically opposed concepts. Nowhere can it ever be observed that the believers lied against Allah and His Messenger in the Age of Hap-piness. Referring to such state of affairs, Abdullah ibn Abbas (d. 687 CE) summarized the situation after the appearance of discord saying that former-ly, upon hearing someone say, "The Messenger of Allah said," they would immediately pay heed. But when falsehood emerged and people competed in narrating the hadith, they would not accept from people except that of which they were assured.[17]

On no account were the hypocrites allowed to lie and thus mix anything into the religion. The Messenger of Allah had disclosed the names of the hyp-ocrites to his Companion Hudhayfa ibn al-Yaman. After the Prophet's de-parture from this world, the Caliphs relied upon Hudhayfa's testimony and adjusted themselves in accordance with his opinions and even his gestures and behavior. The Rightly-Guided Caliphs, may Allah be pleased with them, and succeeding caliphs did not authorize anyone to freely narrate hadith and tightly regulated hadith transmission.

WORKS RELATED TO FABRICATED HADITH

Fabricated (*mawdu*) hadiths have been compiled into separate books by hadith scholars with a view to serving as a case in point and in order for famed hadith fabricators to be known. If they had not engaged in such an

---

[15] This hadith is perfectly sound (*mutawatir*). It has been narrated by more than seventy Companions.

[16] *Sahih Muslim*, Muqaddima, 3

[17] *Sahih Muslim*, Muqaddima, 4

endeavor, we would not have been aware of these words fabricated in the past, for people's informally spreading words of their own invention carries no weight with respect to scholarly activity. For instance, information pertaining to medicine that is spread colloquially is of no significance, and is even forgotten over time, unless it is accepted and documented by physicians. Similarly, it is not possible for knowledge that is not embraced by its specialists to hold any weight.

EVALUATION

1. Define weak hadith.

2. What are the types of weak hadith?

3. What are the ten characteristics disqualifying hadith narrators? (*Mata'in al-ashara*)?

4. What is the ruling concerning weak hadith?

UNIT FIVE

INTENTION, SINCERITY

عَنْ عُمَرَ رَضِيَ اللهُ عَنهُ قال: قَالَ رَسُولُ اللهِ صَلَّى اللهُ عَلَيْهِ وَسَلَّمَ: إِنَّمَا

الْأَعْمَالُ بِالنِّيَّاتِ وَإِنَّمَا لِكُلِّ امْرِئٍ مَا نَوَى، فَمَنْ كَانَتْ هِجْرَتُهُ إِلَى اللهِ

وَرَسُولِهِ فَهِجْرَتُهُ إِلَى اللهِ وَرَسُولِهِ، وَمَنْ كَانَتْ هِجْرَتُهُ إِلَى دُنْيَا يُصِيبُهَا

أَوِ امْرَأَةٍ يَنْكِحُهَا فَهِجْرَتُهُ إِلَى مَا هَاجَرَ إِلَيْهِ.

TRANSLATION

"It is related from Umar ibn al-Khattab, may Allah be pleased with him, that the Messenger of Allah, may Allah bless him and grant him peace, said, "Actions are judged according to intentions. One is rewarded for whatever one intends to do. Whoever emigrates for Allah and His Messenger has emigrated for Allah and His Messenger; whoever emigrates to acquire something worldly or to marry has emigrated for what is intended." (*Sahih al-Bukhari*, Iman, 41; *Sahih Muslim*, Imara, 155).

NARRATOR

Umar ibn al-Khattab

a) Umar, may Allah be pleased with him, embraced Islam in the sixth year of the Prophethood of Allah's Messenger, peace and blessings be upon him. **b)** He is among those Companions promised Paradise. **c)** He was given the name *Faruq*, meaning the Distinguisher Between Truth and Falsehood. **d)** He emigrated to Medina not in secret, but before the very eyes of the Meccan polytheists, in open defiance of them, and was the first person to openly declare his acceptance of Islam. **e)** He became Muslim after the noble Prophet's making the following supplication: "O Allah, strengthen Islam with which of those two, namely, Umar ibn al-Khattab and Amr ibn al-Hisham (Abu Jahl), is more pleasing to You." **f)** He was appointed Caliph following Abu Bakr's caliphate, in the thirteenth year after the Emigration, with his caliphate continuing for ten and a half years. **g)** He was exceptionally fair and right-minded. He would entreat Allah for a verse to be revealed in relation to a particular matter and a verse would immediately be revealed concerning it. **h)** He was assassinated by Persian slave Abu Lu'lu'a in the twenty-third year after the Emigration (Hijra).

EXPLANATION

During the Emigration, all the Muslims were emigrating from Mecca to Medina for the sake of Allah. However, a Companion unknown by name had emigrated to marry a woman he loved, by the name of Umm Qays. This individual too was, without question, a believer, but his intention and purpose did not outweigh his behavior and actions.

He also was one of the Emigrants, but his emigration was to Umm Qays. He endured all this difficulty that could only have been endured for the sake of Allah, for the sake of a woman instead. This incident, without mention of the name of the Companion, became the subject of the above-mentioned Prophetic statement. The particularity of the reason for its articulation does not hinder the universality of the principle. The hadith's ruling, therefore, is general and encompasses all affairs and people.

Allah the Almighty has declared: *"Say (to the believers): 'Whether you keep secret what is in your bosoms or reveal it, Allah knows it. He knows whatever is in the heavens and whatever is on the earth. Allah has full power over everything'"* (Al Imran 3:29).

Secrecy or openness pertains only to human beings. Just as Allah knows all that human beings do when in private, He is also aware of the thoughts and feelings occurring to their hearts. A person who believes in Allah and embraces the religion He revealed, must keep check of their behavior and even the feelings occurring to their hearts. Intention transpires in the heart. If a person senses a lapse in the sincere intention they entertain in their heart, they must renew their intention at once.

This hadith, generally speaking, encompasses the following two topics: Intention and Emigration.

A. INTENTION

1) Imam Ahmad ibn Hanbal said, "The foundations of Islam are upon these three hadith: 'Actions are by intentions'; 'Whoever introduces into this affair of ours that which is not in accordance with it will have it rejected'; and 'The lawful is clear and the prohibited is clear.'"

2) The intention of a believer is better than their deeds. In another hadith, Allah's Messenger, peace and blessings be upon him, said, "Allah considers not your bodily statures, but your hearts. Rather, He considers your hearts."

3) Through their intention, a person's mundane, daily actions become transformed into worship and an entire life becomes meritorious and filled with reward.

4) Whoever intends to carry out an act of goodness, they attain the rewards for having done so even if they are unable to actualize it.

5) Intention is the spirit of deed. That is to say, in the same way that a body without a spirit is of no avail, a deed performed without regard to Divine approval resembles a soulless body and is nothing more than mere display. In one of his hadith, the Messenger of Allah, peace and blessings be upon him, refers to a martyr being the first of people against whom judgment will be pronounced on the Day of Judgment. Upon Allah's calling him to account concerning what he did in the world, he will say, "I fought for You until I died a martyr." The following communication will then take place:

> He [Allah] will say: "You have lied—you did but fight that it might be said [of you]: 'He is courageous.'" And so it was said. Then he will be ordered to be dragged along on his face until he is cast into Hellfire. [Another] will be a man who has studied [religious] knowledge and has taught it and who used to recite the Qur'an. He will be brought and Allah will make known to him His favors and he will recognize them. [The Almighty] will say: "And what did you do about them?" He will say: "I studied [religious] knowledge and I taught it and I recited the Qur'an for Your sake." He will say: "You have lied—you did but study [religious] knowledge that it

might be said [of you]: 'He is learned.'" And you recited the
Qur'an that it might be said [of you]: 'He is a reciter.' And so it
was said. Then he will be ordered to be dragged along on his face
until he is cast into Hellfire.

The continuation of the hadith gives an account of a wealthy man
who will be brought to account who will say that he spent it for
Allah's sake. He too will be told that he did so that it might be said
of him, "He is open-handed." And he too will be ordered to be
dragged along on his face until he is cast into Hellfire (*Sahih Muslim*, Imara, 152).

6) Intention holds such excellence that it transforms sin into reward and
   reward into sin. That is to say, intention is a spirit and the spirit of
   that spirit is sincerity. On this account, salvation is only possible with
   sincerity.

B. EMIGRATION

وَمَنْ يُهَاجِرْ فِى سَبِيلِ اللهِ يَجِدْ فِى الْاَرْضِ مُرَاغَماً كَثِيراً وَسَعَةً وَمَنْ
يَخْرُجْ مِنْ بَيْتِهِ مُهَاجِراً اِلَى اللهِ وَرَسُولِهِ ثُمَّ يُدْرِكْهُ الْمَوْتُ فَقَدْ وَقَعَ
اَجْرُهُ عَلَى اللهِ وَكَانَ اللهُ غَفُوراً رَحِيماً

Whoever emigrates in Allah's cause will find on the earth enough room
for refuge and plentiful resources. He who leaves his home as an emigrant to Allah and His Messenger, and whom death overtakes (while still
on the way), his reward is due and sure with Allah. Assuredly, Allah is
All-Forgiving, All- Compassionate. (an-Nisa 4:100)

Definition: Emigration literally means to abandon and to leave one
place to settle in another.

In a religious context, emigration denotes a person's leaving the country or region in which they reside, to settle in another, in the event of their
inability to freely practice their religion due to oppression and persecution.

Historically speaking, the Emigration is the emigration of the Prophet and his Companions from Mecca to Medina in the year 622.

Intention is of utmost importance in emigration, If emigration is realized in order to earn Allah's approval and good pleasure, then the reward mentioned in the following Prophetic Tradition can be attained: "If anyone leaves their home for (the sake of) Allah and something befalls them on the way, the angels cannot record their reward; it is Allah Who will reward him." Otherwise it will amount to nothing other than sightseeing or being wearied by travel. All the Prophets have emigrated, including Prophet Ibrahim, Prophet Isa, and Prophet Muhammad, peace be upon them.

The Messenger of Allah, peace and blessings be upon him, states, "Whosoever seeks martyrdom with sincerity will be ranked by Allah among the martyrs even if they die in their bed."

Sincerity is to undertake everything one does with complete belief and to perfection, on account of Allah's having commanded it.

Emigration is of Two Kinds:

a) **Emigration from Sin**, or the abandonment of wrongdoing. The best emigrant is one who emigrates from sin and transgression. Leaving behind those things that Allah has prohibited is considered to be emigration in the general sense. Thus, Allah's Messenger, peace and blessings be upon him, states, "The emigrant (*muhajir*) is one who abandons what Allah has forbidden."

b) **Emigration to Allah's Mercy:** This refers to immediately abandoning a sin after having committed it, turning to Allah's mercy, and entreating His forgiveness. It is echoing the words of Ibrahim ibn Adham and beseeching Allah's mercy and forgiveness: "O Allah, Your rebellious servant has come to Your door. He knows that his sins are great, but nevertheless entreats You. If You forgive him, this is from Your majesty. If You turn him away, he has no other door to which to turn."

The noble Messenger stated, "There is no emigration after the Conquest of Mecca," but this is in terms of emigration from Mecca to Medina. That is to say, emigration continues in our day, and every journey or flight from one's land and home undertaken for the sake of Allah still constitutes an emigration and, provided one's intention is sincere, one attains the rewards of emigration.

LESSONS FROM THE HADITH

1. In order to obtain reward from deeds undertaken, it is essential that these be undertaken with good intention. **2.** Due to the importance of intention being realized with the heart, it is not necessary to verbalize this with the tongue. **3.** Actions carried out without any regard to Divine pleasure and approval cannot be meritorious. **4.** A person must appear as they are and not exploit religion for their own ends. **5.** Sincerity denotes soundness of intention.

EVALUATION

1. When did Umar, may Allah be pleased with him, embrace Islam and what is his title?
2. What is the reason for the communication of the hadith?
3. What is better for a believer than their deeds?
4. According to which characteristic does Allah judge human beings?
5. To which organ is the soundness or corruption of a person's other bodily organs connected?
6. Considering Allah's granting us eternal life in Paradise is not dependent upon our deeds, what will it depend upon?
7. Why will Allah cast certain people into Hellfire who will assert that they were martyred, learned the Qur'an, acquired knowledge, and spent their wealth in His Name?
8. What is the secret that transforms sins into rewards and rewards into sins?
9. What is the literal and technical meaning of emigration?

10. How is a person to be recorded among the emigrants if they are unable

to emigrate and die instead in their own country?

11. What are the other two types of emigration?

12. What are the characteristics of an ideal emigrant?

13. What kinds of lessons can be learned from the hadith on intention?

UNIT SIX

IMAN, ISLAM, *IHSAN*

عَنْ عُمَرَ بْنِ الْخَطَّابِ رَضِيَ اللهُ عَنه قَالَ: بَيْنَمَا نَحْنُ جُلُوسٌ عِنْدَ رَسُولِ اللهِ صَلَّى اللهُ عَلَيْهِ وَسَلَّمَ ذَاتَ يَوْمٍ إِذْ طَلَعَ عَلَيْنَا رَجُلٌ شَدِيدُ بَيَاضِ الثِّيَابِ شَدِيدُ سَوَادِ الشَّعْرِ، لَا يُرَى عَلَيْهِ أَثَرُ السَّفَرِ، وَلَا يَعْرِفُهُ مِنَّا أَحَدٌ، حَتَّى جَلَسَ إِلَى النَّبِيِّ، فَأَسْنَدَ رُكْبَتَيْهِ إِلَى رُكْبَتَيْهِ وَوَضَعَ كَفَّيْهِ عَلَى فَخِذَيْهِ وَقَالَ: يَا مُحَمَّدُ أَخْبِرْنِي عَنِ الْإِسْلَامِ فَقَالَ رَسُولُ اللهِ: الْإِسْلَامُ أَنْ تَشْهَدَ أَنْ لَا إِلَهَ إِلَّا اللهُ وَأَنَّ مُحَمَّدًا رَسُولُ اللهِ وَتُقِيمَ الصَّلَاةَ وَتُؤْتِيَ الزَّكَاةَ وَتَصُومَ رَمَضَانَ وَتَحُجَّ الْبَيْتَ إِنِ اسْتَطَعْتَ إِلَيْهِ سَبِيلاً. قَالَ: صَدَقْتَ. فَعَجِبْنَا لَهُ يَسْأَلُهُ وَيُصَدِّقُهُ، قَالَ: فَأَخْبِرْنِي عَنِ الْإِيمَانِ. قَالَ: أَنْ تُؤْمِنَ بِاللهِ وَمَلَائِكَتِهِ وَكُتُبِهِ وَرُسُلِهِ وَالْيَوْمِ الْآخِرِ وَتُؤْمِنَ بِالْقَدَرِ خَيْرِهِ وَشَرِّهِ. قَالَ: صَدَقْتَ قَالَ: فَأَخْبِرْنِي عَنِ الْإِحْسَانِ. قَالَ: أَنْ تَعْبُدَ اللهَ كَأَنَّكَ تَرَاهُ، فَإِنْ لَمْ تَكُنْ تَرَاهُ فَإِنَّهُ يَرَاكَ، قَالَ: فَأَخْبِرْنِي عَنِ السَّاعَةِ. قَالَ: مَا الْمَسْؤُولُ عَنْهَا بِأَعْلَمَ مِنَ السَّائِلِ. قَالَ: فَأَخْبِرْنِي عَنْ أَمَارَاتِهَا. قَالَ أَنْ تَلِدَ الْأَمَةُ رَبَّتَهَا، وَأَنْ تَرَى الْحُفَاةَ الْعُرَاةَ الْعَالَةَ رِعَاءَ الشَّاءِ يَتَطَاوَلُونَ فِي الْبُنْيَانِ ثُمَّ انْطَلَقَ، فَلَبِثْتُ مَلِيًّا، ثُمَّ قَالَ: يَا عُمَرُ أَتَدْرِي مَنِ السَّائِلُ؟ قُلْتُ: اللهُ وَرَسُولُهُ أَعْلَمُ قَالَ: فَإِنَّهُ جِبْرِيلُ أَتَاكُمْ يُعَلِّمُكُمْ دِينَكُمْ.

TRANSLATION

Umar ibn al-Khattab, may Allah be pleased with him, reports:
"We were sitting with Allah's Messenger, upon him be peace and blessings, when there appeared a man before us a man whose clothes were exceedingly white, whose hair was exceedingly black, upon whom traces of travelling could not be seen, and whom none of us knew. He sat down close to the Prophet, may Allah bless him and grant him

peace, so that he rested his knees upon his knees and placed his two hands upon his thighs and said:

'Muhammad! Tell me about Islam.' Allah's Messenger, upon him be peace and blessings, said: 'Islam is that you witness that there is no deity but Allah and that Muhammad is His Messenger, and you establish the Prayer, and you give the *zakah* (prescribed annual alms), and you fast (during the month of) Ramadan, and you perform the hajj (pilgrimage) to the House if you are able to find a way to it.'

He said, 'You have told the truth,' and we were amazed at him asking him and [then] telling him that he told the truth. He said, 'Tell me about belief (*iman*).' He (the Messenger of Allah) said: 'That you affirm Allah, His angels, His Books, His Messengers, and the Last Day, and that you affirm the Decree, the good of it and the bad of it.'

He said, 'You have told the truth.' He said, 'Tell me about ihsan (perfect goodness).' He said: 'That you worship Allah as if you see Him, for although you cannot see Him, truly He sees you.'

He said, 'Tell me about the Hour.' He said: 'The one asked about it knows no more than the one asking.' He said, 'Then tell me about its signs.' He said, 'That the female slave should give birth to her mistress, and you see poor, naked, barefoot shepherds of sheep and goats competing in raising tall buildings.'

He went away, and I remained some time. Then he (Allah's Messenger) asked: 'O Umar, do you know who the questioner was?' I said, 'Allah and His Messenger know best.' He said: 'He was Jabrail. He came to you to teach you your religion.'" (*Sahih Muslim*, Iman, 1).

Note: Refer to Unit Five for further information on Umar ibn al-Kattab, may Allah be pleased with him, the narrator of this hadith.

EXPLANATION OF THE HADITH

a. Archangel Jabrail's appearing before the Messenger of Allah, peace and blessings be upon him, and asking questions was for the purpose of teaching the Companions their religion.

b. This hadith came to pass near the time of the Prophet's demise, as the Pilgrimage became obligatory after the conquest of Mecca and the Pilgrimage has been listed among the pillars of Islam mentioned herein.

c. The questions directed to the Prophet in the hadiths have been asked rather methodologically. Due to its externals, Islam has been inquired about first, followed by belief—which pertains to the inner world or heart entirely—and later perfect goodness, or *ihsan*, the highest degree of belief.

To the question concerning the Last Day, the Messenger of Allah, peace and blessings be upon him, replied that he did not know. However, it was Archangel Jabrail who had previously communicated to the Prophet, via Divine revelation, that he ought to reply in such a way to this question, and he knew that Allah's Messenger, peace and blessings be upon him, would reply in this way. In that case, why did he ask?

His reasons for asking this question are the following:

• To demonstrate to all others that this matter was among the Divine secrets and that even the Prophet himself could not acquire knowledge in this regard, without the permission of Allah.

• Through this response, the Messenger of Allah, peace and blessings be upon him, illustrated before all those Companions, despite being a Prophet, just how connected he was to truth; at the same time, he demonstrated that a person cannot know everything and that it was not shameful or damaging to one's pride to admit that one does not know something.

IMAN AND ISLAM

1) **Iman:** Verbal profession and confirmation with the heart. This signifies the heart's affirming what the tongue utters. Accordingly, if the heart fails to affirm what the tongue declares, a person cannot be considered to have believed in the complete sense, even if they per-

form their worship outwardly. In any case, such people are referred to as hypocrites (*munafiqun*) in Islam.

2) In this hadith, the Messenger of Allah, peace and blessings be upon him, has referred to the aspects of religion pertaining to the heart as *iman* and those concerning practice, or deeds, as *Islam*.

3) Imam Zuhri states: "Islam is word, while *iman* is deed." In other words, Islam must be understood in the literal sense. Belief, however, is praxis and implementation.

IHSAN

1. The literal meaning of *ihsan* is twofold: The word denotes doing something well and to perfection; it also comes to mean doing what is beautiful and good to others.

The aspect of perfect goodness in this sense, which looks to human beings, is represented in the principle, "Wish for others what you wish for yourself." The universal dimension which encompasses all creatures is explained in the hadith, "Verily Allah has prescribed *ihsan* (excellence, perfection) in all things. So if you kill then kill well and if you slaughter, then slaughter well. Let each one of you sharpen his blade and let him spare suffering to the animal he slaughters."

The Qur'anic verse, "*Is the recompense of excellence (in obedience to Allah) other than excellence?*" (ar-Rahman 55:60) evokes this meaning. On one occasion, the Prophet had recited this verse and asked his Companions:

"Do you know what your Lord wills to reveal through this verse?"

Upon their replying, "Allah and His Messenger know best," he said that Allah said, "Can the reward for one whom I favored (in their worldly life) with belief in Divine Unity, be other than Paradise?"

2. Allah has decreed the following in relation to perfect goodness:

Allah enjoins justice (and right judgment in all matters), and devotion to doing good, and generosity towards relatives, and He forbids you indecency, wickedness and vile conduct (all offenses against religion, life, personal property, chastity, and health of mind and body). He exhorts you (repeatedly) so that you may reflect and be mindful! (an-Nahl 16:90)

SIGNS OF THE LAST DAY

1. That the female slave should give birth to her mistress:

Implied here is that there will come such a time, towards the Last Day, in which children will be undutiful, disrespectful and unloving towards their parents. They will not show them the required love and benevolence and will not observe the rights of parents. They will perpetrate unimaginable evil towards their parents, to whom Allah prohibited even the saying of "Ugh!" (as an indication of complaint or impatience).

Another noteworthy point in the text of the hadith is the Messenger's use of the feminine *rabbata* (mistress). This illustrates that the child being born is female. So confused will everything become that even daughters, who normally have a closer relationship of reciprocal love and compassion with their mothers, will mistreat their mothers. Allah and His Messenger know best.

2. ...and you see poor, naked, barefoot shepherds of sheep and goats competing in raising tall buildings:

There will come such a time when people who are unqualified and incompetent will reach high positions with their money. They will become police officers, ministers, doctors, and the like. They will, as such, violate the rights of others and misdirect and mismanage government, and corruption, theft, and deception will increase.

LESSONS FROM THE HADITH

1. Angels can appear in human form. They can speak, and human beings can hear their speech. **2.** *Iman* constitutes accepting the essentials of belief, while Islam is putting the rules prescribed by the religion into practice in one's life. **3.** A person's openly declaring the Declaration of Faith is necessary in way of their being accepted as Muslim. **4.** The question-and-answer method is an effective technique in education and teaching. **5.** Respect to scholars and assemblies of learning is elemental. **6.** Knowledge of the Last day rests only with Allah. **7.** Affairs being placed in the hands of those unqualified to undertake them, the increase of disobedience, and the disintegration of the family institution are signs of the Last Day. **8.** A Muslim must always act in the consciousness of responsibility. **9.** Perfect goodness and self-supervision (*muraqaba*) are of two degrees: The servant's living their life "as if seeing Allah," is the first degree. "Knowing that He sees them though they do not see Him" constitutes the second degree.

EVALUATION

1. How did the Messenger of Allah, peace and blessings be upon him, describe perfect goodness when asked by Archangel Jabrail?
2. What could be the wisdom behind Jabrail's addressing the Prophet by name, as did some of the unlettered Arabs of the time?
3. Why did Jabrail ask the Prophet the question regarding the Hour, despite knowing what his answer would be?
4. What is the meaning of *iman*?
5. What is the generally accepted view concerning *iman* and *Islam* being either synonymous or not? Who espoused this view?
6. What is the literal meaning of *ihsan*?
7. What are the dimensions of *ihsan* which look to human beings and all creation?
8. What will be the recompense for *ihsan*?
9. Allah enjoins ...., and devotion to doing good, and generosity towards ...., and He .... you ...., wickedness and vile conduct. He exhorts you (repeatedly) so that you may reflect and be mindful!
10. What was Prophet Joseph's response to Zulaykha as to why he had escaped her?
11. What are the signs of the Last Day mentioned in the hadith?
12. What does a slave's giving birth to her mistress imply?
13. What is the meaning of "poor, naked, barefoot shepherds of sheep and goats competing in raising tall buildings"?

UNIT SEVEN

REPENTANCE, SEEKING

FORGIVENESS

عَنِ الْأَغَرِّ بْنِ يَسَارٍ الْمُزَنِيِّ قَالَ: قَالَ رَسُولُ اللهِ: يَا أَيُّهَا النَّاسُ
تُوبُوا إِلَى اللهِ وَاسْتَغْفِرُوهُ فَإِنِّي أَتُوبُ فِي الْيَوْمِ مِائَةَ مَرَّةٍ.

TRANSLATION

Al-Agharr ibn Yasar al-Muzani, may Allah be pleased with him, said that the Messenger of Allah, may Allah bless him and grant him peace, said: "O people! Turn in repentance towards Allah and ask His forgiveness. I turn towards Him a hundred times a day." (*Sahih Muslim*, Dhikr, 42; *Sunan Abu Dawud*, Witr, 26).

NARRATOR

Al-Agharr ibn Yasar al-Muzani

a) Al-Agharr ibn Yasar al-Muzani, may Allah be pleased with him, was among the first to emigrate to Medina. **b)** He is also known by the name Al-Juhani. **c)** Ibn Umar, Mu'awiya ibn Qurra, and Abu Burda have related hadith from him. **d)** He has narrated three hadith, two of them on the subject of repentance and seeking forgiveness from Allah.

EXPLANATION

1. As the hadith begins with the expression "O people," it can be understood that all human beings have been summoned to repentance and seeking forgiveness.

2. **Repentance and seeking forgiveness:** Denotes a person's recognizing their own self and their shortcomings as well as their Lord and His Greatness and, as such, their seeking spiritual ascension. Abdullah ibn Umar, may Allah be pleased with him, reports that he heard the Prophet, peace and blessings be upon him, asking Allah to forgive him a hundred times in an assembly with the words, "O Allah, forgive me, pardon me and show mercy to me, for You are the Oft-Relent-

ing, All-Compassionate," and that they too used to repeat this. As there can be no one who is superior in rank to the Prophet, everyone is in need of repentance.

3. Allah declares, "...*Surely Allah loves those who turn to Him in sincere repentance (of past sins and errors), and He loves those who cleanse themselves*" (al-Baqarah 2:222). In any event, repentance is a form of purification of the heart. It is the heart's being cleansed of the black stains enveloping it.

According to a narration of Abu Hamza Anas ibn Malik al-Ansari, the Messenger of Allah, upon him be peace and blessings, said:

"Allah is happier with repentance of His slave than one of you who loses his camel in the desert and then comes upon it (unexpectedly)." *Sahih al-Bukhari*, Da'awat, 4; *Sahih Muslim*, Tawbah 1, 7, 8.

4. Human beings are born into the world without sin and impurity. Subsequently deviating from this pure and straight path for a number of reasons, they thrust themselves into the dust of transgression and waste away therein. Indeed, sins are the means throwing human beings by the wayside and causing their ruin. In regard to a person's turning to Allah once again after wrongdoing, the Qur'an states, "Turn to your Lord in penitence and submit to Him wholly." Such being the case, repentance is a person's immediate cleansing and a return to their essence, after having lost their purity. It is stated in a hadith: "When the believer commits sin, a black spot appears on his heart. If he repents and gives up that sin and seeks forgiveness, his heart will be purified and polished. But if he increases in sin, the blackness increases." In other words, the idea of committing sin becomes impressed upon them.

5. Another aspect of repentance is a person's desiring the best in relation to their carnal self by not ever returning to their former wrongdoing and thus not allowing it to distance itself from Allah. That is why they ought to be resolute, from the outset, not to commit sin

and, when considering their carnal self in relation to their sins, must accept its pulling away from Allah as so great a crime as to be unforgivable. Allah has promised that He will forgive everything save the association of partners with Him[18]. Thus, it can be said that one must not remain where one has fallen, but take action at once; one must turn to Allah, repent for former sins committed and, in so doing, strive to rediscover oneself anew. This is what can be referred to as the sincere, true repentance, or *tawbah an-nasuh*.

Conditions for a True Repentance:

The first: If the sin committed concerns the rights of others, one must first approach the person whose rights have been violated and seek pardon from them.

The second: One must display strong resolve and commitment not to return to that same sin.

The third: Time must not be allowed to elapse between that sin and repentance and one must repent without delay.

The fourth: Shedding tears and weeping due to one's sins is essential. Tears extinguish the Fire.

6. The world of today, with its streets and centers of attraction and amusement, has been transformed into a sea of sin. In our day, Satan or his accomplices from among human beings or the jinn are far and wide, lying in wait at every corner for the victims to fall into their clutches. Every believer in such a society must act with the awareness that, "In every sin, there is a path that leads to disbelief." When a person commits a sin, they must express their deep sorrow at having erred thus and take refuge in their Lord, exclaiming, "O Lord, I know not how I could have done this! I stand before You in utter shame for what I have done."

Our wrongdoing can be forgiven through our shedding tears due to the sins we have committed; this is because tears put out the flames of Hellfire.

---

[18] An-Nisa 4:48

LESSONS TO BE LEARNED

1. While repentance is not restricted to a particular numerical value, we must repent and ask Allah's forgiveness at least one hundred times each day. **2.** Allah is most compassionate towards His servants. He is ready to forgive them in the event of their seeking His forgiveness. **3.** Every difficulty is followed by ease and there is comfort at the end of every hardship. As a matter of course, a person must never despair in the mercy and compassion of their Lord. **4.** A person must constantly hold themselves to account and repent sincerely for their sins. **5.** Allah forgives the sins that a person commits unwittingly. And so, a man reunited with his camel mistakenly exclaiming out of his boundless joy, "O Lord, You are my servant and I am Your Lord," —as mentioned in a narration—has not been regarded as a sin.

EVALUATION

1. According to hadith, how many times did the Prophet repent each day?
2. What is the meaning of repentance and seeking forgiveness?
3. To what has the Prophet likened Allah's delight at a servant's repentance?
4. What state does the heart assume as the servant commits sin?
5. What is "true repentance" and what are its conditions?
6. What can each sin contain?
7. What qualities must repentance have?
8. How did Ibrahim ibn Adham seek forgiveness from Allah?
9. The eyes of which two persons will not witness the fire of Hell?
10. What can extinguish the fire of Hell for a believer?
11. Why did Satan wake Mu'awiya for the Prayer?

UNIT EIGHT

PATIENCE

عَنْ صُهَيْبِ بْنِ سِنَانٍ قَالَ: قَالَ رَسُولُ اللهِ صَلَّى اللهُ عَلَيْهِ وَسَلَّمَ: "عَجَبًا
لِأَمْرِ الْمُؤْمِنِ إِنَّ أَمْرَهُ كُلَّهُ لَهُ خَيْرٌ، وَلَيْسَ ذَلِكَ لِأَحَدٍ إِلَّا لِلْمُؤْمِنِ؛ إِنْ
أَصَابَتْهُ سَرَّاءُ شَكَرَ فَكَانَ خَيْرًا لَهُ وَإِنْ أَصَابَتْهُ ضَرَّاءُ صَبَرَ فَكَانَ خَيْرًا لَهُ".

TRANSLATION

S uhayb ibn Sinan, may Allah be well pleased with him, reported that the Messenger of Allah, may Allah bless him and grant him peace, said: "How wonderful is the situation of the believer, for all his affairs are good, and such a condition is only for a believer. If something good happens to him he gives thanks, and that is good for him; if something bad happens to him he bears it with patience, and that is also good for him." (*Sahih Muslim*, Zuhd, 64).

NARRATOR

Suhayb ibn Sinan

a) Suahyb ibn Sinan, may Allah be pleased with him, is a Companion famous with the name Suhayb al-Rumi. b) Learning Islam from Ammar ibn Yasir, he became Muslim at once. c) Giving everything that he had to the Meccan polytheists, he emigrated to Medina suffering a thousand and one difficulties. d) Highly proficient at shooting with a bow and arrow, Suhayb participated in all battles alongside Allah's Messenger, peace and blessings be upon him. e) At the time Umar, may Allah be pleased with him, was assassinated, he acted as interim caliph for a period of three days upon the caliph's request. f) He passed away at the age of seventy-three, in the thirty-eighth year after the Emigration, and was buried in Medina's Al-Baqi Cemetery.

May Allah be well pleased with him.

EXPLANATION

1. In this hadith, the Messenger of Allah, peace and blessings be upon him, draws attention to the favorable situation of the believer, in which all their affairs are good and felicitous and thus invites believers to patience and thankfulness.

Life continues with its highs and its lows. Becoming spoilt when one experiences joy and unmeasured grief in the face of sorrow can adversely affect a believer and lead them to great error. The believer is delivered from this hazardous situation through thankfulness for bounties and patience in the face of hardship.

2. Allah the Almighty declares:

$$ وَلَنَبْلُوَنَّكُمْ بِشَيْءٍ مِنَ الْخَوْفِ وَالْجُوعِ وَنَقْصٍ مِنَ الْاَمْوَالِ وَالْاَنْفُسِ وَالثَّمَرَاتِ وَبَشِّرِ الصَّابِرِينَ $$

> We will certainly test you with something of fear and hunger, and loss of wealth and lives and fruits (earnings); but give glad tidings to the persevering and patient. (al-Baqarah 2:155).

It is declared in another verse:

$$ اَلَّذِينَ اِذَا ذُكِرَ اللهُ وَجِلَتْ قُلُوبُهُمْ وَالصَّابِرِينَ عَلٰى مَا اَصَابَهُمْ وَالْمُقِيمِى الصَّلٰوةِ وَمِمَّا رَزَقْنَاهُمْ يُنْفِقُونَ $$

> Those whose hearts tremble with awe whenever Allah is mentioned, who are always patient with whatever ill befalls them, who always establish the Prayer in conformity with its conditions, and who spend (in Allah's cause and for the needy) out of whatever we provide for them. (al-Hajj 22:35)

3. Types of Patience: **a)** Patience in the face of misfortune; **b)** Patience in avoiding sins; **c)** Patience in observing regular acts of worship; and **d)** Patience in relation to time.

a) Patience in the face of misfortune: Misfortune encompasses the various difficulties and hardship that a person can meet throughout their lives, such as illness, death and the like.

Strictly speaking, a person must accept the misfortunes befalling them as being from themselves and consider where and how they went wrong that this evil befell them. They must call themselves to account and perpetually keep themselves in check. In other words, if a person seeks to correct their errors, they must act as a prosecutor to their own carnal self and a defense attorney to others. A believer knows that whatever evil befalls them, it is from themselves and whatever good happens to them is from Allah; they are thus patient when misfortune strikes and thankful and humble when they receive goodness.

Consequently, the standard of a believer must always be Divine approval and they must do whatever is right and leave the outcome to Allah, in perfect reliance upon him. Allah the Almighty declares:

وَعَسَى اَنْ تَكْرَهُوا شَيْئاً وَهُوَ خَيْرٌ لَكُمْ وَعَسَى اَنْ تُحِبُّوا شَيْئاً وَهُوَ

شَرٌّ لَكُمْ وَاللهُ يَعْلَمُ وَاَنْتُمْ لَا تَعْلَمُونَ

> ...It may well be that you dislike a thing but it is good for you, and it may well be that you like a thing but it is bad for you. Allah knows, and you do not know. (al-Baqarah 2:216)

Human beings have no right of complaint in tribulation and illness.

1) Life is cleansed and strengthened, bears fruit and achieves completion with tribulations and illness.

2) This world is an arena of trial and examination and is the site of service. It is not the site of pleasure, merit and reward. One hour of patience during times of illness enables a person to earn the reward of one day's worship.

b) Patience in avoiding sins: A person must respond with the same patience to those things that Allah has prohibited. Patience to be shown upon the first emergence of sin averts the evil to come from it and the person thus staves off its blow. It is for this reason that the Messenger of Allah, peace and blessings be upon him, said to Ali, may Allah be pleased with him, "O Ali, the first glance is in your favor, but the second is against you." In other words, one's gaze can fall upon the forbidden, but if they immediately avert their gaze, this is not recorded as a sin in their name.

c) Patience in observing regular acts of worship: Patience is vital in constant and regular worship of Allah. For a person who is only just beginning to observe the Prescribed Prayer, this act of worship can seem quite onerous at the first instance; however, if they are patient and if their spirit becomes one with the Prayer, any Prayer missed thereafter becomes a source of the greatest sorrow for them. The same can be said of such acts of worship as fasting, offering the prescribed annual alms, and the Pilgrimage. Consider the fact that those who undertake an act of worship as arduous as the Pilgrimage wish to return each year. At times, even the quotas placed on the number of people attending disturb them immensely. This love of worship in a sense implies their overcoming their initial exertion. This is the same for virtually all forms of worship.

d) Patience in relation to time: This is the type of patience that a person needs to show towards affluence and poverty. One must not question why they are poor while another is wealthy, but must be patient and work. They must not show haste in realizing hopes or plans that require a certain length of time to achieve.

WHAT WE HAVE LEARNED

1. Belief is not a barrier to affliction and hardship. **2.** Hardship can be transformed into bounty through patience. **3.** Just as thankfulness for a bounty is a means for its increase, patience in the face of affliction can be a means for its transformation into goodness. **4.** Thankfulness and patience provide the opportunity to spend one's entire life upon goodness.

EVALUATION

1. What does a believer do when they are happy and when affliction be-
    falls them?

2. Write three characteristics of Suhayb ibn Sinan.

3. How does Allah describe the qualities of believers in the Qur'anic chap-
    ter Hajj, verse 35?

4. How many types of patience are there? What are these?

5. What should a person do if they want to straighten their errors?

6. Human beings have no right of complaint during misfortune and illness
    in three respects. List these.

7. What has the Prophet said in relation to looking at the forbidden?

8. What are the four essentials leading to a person's happiness and success
    enumerated in Surah al-Asr?

9. Which individual became resolved to pursue his studies to become a
    great scholar after observing that water wears away the hardest stone?

10. What lessons can be taken from this hadith?

UNIT NINE

MUHASABA – MURAQABA

(Self-Criticism and Self-Supervision)

عَنْ أَبِي يَعْلَى، شَدَّادِ بْنِ أَوْسٍ قَالَ: قَالَ رَسُولُ اللهِ صَلَّى اللهُ عَلَيْهِ

وَسَلَّمَ: الْكَيِّسُ مَنْ دَانَ نَفْسَهُ وَعَمِلَ لِمَا بَعْدَ الْمَوْتِ وَالْعَاجِزُ مَنْ

أَتْبَعَ نَفْسَهُ هَوَاهَا ثُمَّ تَمَنَّى عَلَى اللهِ.

TRANSLATION

Abu Ya'la ibn Shaddad ibn Aws, may Allah be well pleased with him, narrates that the Messenger of Allah, may Allah bless him and grant him peace, said: "A wise person is one who keeps a watch over his bodily desires and passions, and checks himself from that which is harmful and strives for that which will benefit him after death; and a foolish person is one who subordinates himself to his cravings and desires and expects from Allah the fulfillment of his futile desires." (*Sunan at-Tirmidhi*, Qiyama, 25; See also: *Sunan ibn Majah*, Zuhd, 31).

NARRATOR

Shaddad ibn Aws

a) Shaddad ibn Aws, may Allah be pleased with him, is the child of a Muslim family. **b)** His nickname was Abu Ya'la or Abu Abdu'r-Rahman. **c)** He was superior in terms of knowledge and mildness of character. **d)** He narrated approximately fifty hadith from Allah's Messenger, peace and blessings be upon him. **e)** He passed away at age seventy-five in the fifty-eighth year after the Emigration, in the city of Jerusalem.

EXPLANATION

The indications of wisdom, specified in the hadith as control over one's carnal self and striving for the Hereafter are, to a large extent, connected to a belief that is complete. Control over one's carnal self implies making reason sovereign in one's life. Regulating one's actions in consideration of their repercussions in the Hereafter is the attitude of the wise, in the true sense of the term. The Qur'anic verse, "...*and let every person consider what he has forwarded for the morrow,*" (al-Hashr 69:18) demonstrates just how judicious are the works of those who strive for what will benefit them in their life after death. Moreover, Imam Tirmidhi indicates that the expression translated as "who keeps a watch over his bodily desires and passions" refers to "a person who calls their carnal self to account before it is called to account in the Hereafter." Subsequently, he narrates two views in support of this contention.

Umar, may Allah be pleased with him, has said: "Call yourselves to account before you are called to account." Make preparations for the supreme tribunal. The reckoning in the Hereafter will be easy for those who hold their carnal soul answerable in this world.

An indication of weakness has been regarded in the hadith as subordinating oneself to their carnal desires and fancies and then being in expectation from Allah. Perhaps the sole consolation for those who have become enslaved to their carnal souls is baseless misgiving. The following verses serve as severe caution in this regard:

يَا أَيُّهَا الْإِنْسَانُ مَا غَرَّكَ بِرَبِّكَ الْكَرِيمِ ۞ اَلَّذِى خَلَقَكَ فَسَوّٰيكَ فَعَدَلَكَ ۞ فِى اَىّ صُورَةٍ مَا شَاءَ رَكَّبَكَ

O human! What is it that deludes you concerning your Lord, the All-Munificent? He Who has created you, fashioned you, and proportioned you (in measures perfect for the purpose of your creation); Having constituted you in whatever form He has willed. (al-Infitar 82:6–8).

وَذٰلِكُمْ ظَنُّكُمُ الَّذِى ظَنَنْتُمْ بِرَبِّكُمْ اَرْدٰيكُمْ فَاَصْبَحْتُمْ مِنَ الْخَاسِرِينَ

It is that supposition of yours which you entertained about your Lord that has tumbled you down into perdition, and so you have come to be among the losers. (Fussilat 41:23).

1. Allah describes to us a scene pertaining to the Hereafter as follows:

يَوْمَئِذٍ تُعْرَضُونَ لَا تَخْفٰى مِنْكُمْ خَافِيَةٌ ۞ فَاَمَّا مَنْ اُوتِيَ كِتَابَهُ بِيَمِينِهِ فَيَقُولُ هَاؤُمُ اقْرَؤُا كِتَابِيَهْ ۞ اِنّى ظَنَنْتُ اَنّى مُلَاقٍ حِسَابِيَهْ ۞ فَهُوَ فى عِيشَةٍ رَاضِيَةٍ

> On that day you will be arraigned for judgment, and no secret of yours
> will remain hidden. Then, as for him who is given his record in his right
> hand, he will say: 'Here, take and read my record! I surely knew that
> (one day) I would meet my account.' And so he will be in a state of life
> pleasing to him. (al-Haqqa 69:18–21).

As stated in the verse, a person who is aware while in this world that
they will one day be brought to account for their actions and who checks
themselves accordingly, will not be left stupefied in the Hereafter; their final destination, eternal life in Paradise, will be one with which they are
well pleased and in which they will experience a felicity never-ending. It is
precisely these people of whom Allah's Messenger, peace and blessings be
upon him, speaks as 'the wise' in this hadith.

2. ***Muhasaba***, which denotes reckoning, settling accounts, and self-in-
    terrogation, in a spiritual context signifies the daily self-criticism of a
    believer who, constantly analyzing their deeds and thoughts, re-
    sponds to goodness with thankfulness and strives to remove sins
    with repentance.

3. In view of a remarkable address during one of his sermons, Umar,
    may Allah be pleased with him, interrupted his own address, say-
    ing: "O Umar, you were a shepherd taking care of your father's
    sheep!"

Hasan al-Basri, suckled by one of the wives of the Prophet, is a great
personality. He would interrogate himself every day, saying, "Were you not
the same person who thought of such-and-such in your Prayer the other
day? How could you do such a thing in the presence of your Lord? See
yourself for what you truly are!"

4. How to practice self-criticism:

1. To observe all acts of worship sincerely and earnestly. **2.** To see even one's best acts of worship as wanting. **3.** To hold oneself in contempt before others, and to such an extent that one is in perpetual gratitude towards Allah for not being an unbeliever. **4.** A person who possesses the gift of eloquent speech must not see himself or herself as knowing everything.

WHAT WE HAVE LEARNED

1. Wisdom and foresightedness is reflected in one's behavior. **2.** The delineation between "the wise" and "the foolish" pertains to the situation of evaluating the world and the Hereafter, as well as preparation for life after death. **3.** In order for a person to receive the benefit of Divine assistance, they must do what is necessary to this end: "...*Allah's mercy is indeed near to those devoted to doing good...*" (al-A'raf 7:56) **4.** Allah rewards deeds, not vain desires.

EVALUATION

1. Who is the wise person, according to the hadith?
2. At what age and in what year did Shaddad ibn Aws pass away?
3. How has Imam Tirmidhi described the meaning of the expression, "who keeps a watch over his bodily desires and passions"?
4. Call yourselves to .... before you are .... to ....
5. What is the meaning of 'being deluded in relation to Allah'?
6. What is the literal meaning of *muhasaba*?
7. What did Umar, may Allah be pleased with him, once say during his sermon, so as to overcome his carnal self?
8. What are the necessary criteria for self-criticism?
9. About whom and for which reason did the Prophet utter the following statement: "By Allah, such was the repentance of this woman that were it to be divided among seventy people of Medina, it would suffice"?
10. What lessons can be taken from the hadith?

UNIT TEN

AVOIDING INNOVATION

عَنْ عَائِشَةَ رَضِيَ اللهُ عنها قَالَتْ قَالَ رَسُولُ اللهِ صَلَّى اللهُ
عَلَيْهِ وَسَلَّمَ: مَنْ أَحْدَثَ فِي أَمْرِنَا هٰذَا مَا لَيْسَ مِنْهُ فَهُوَ رَدّ.

TRANSLATION

It is related that Aisha, may Allah be well pleased with her, said that the Messenger of Allah, may Allah bless him and grant him peace, said: "Anyone who introduces an innovation in this affair of ours which is not part of it, that will be rejected."

One version in Muslim reads: "He who does an act which we have not commanded, will have it rejected [by Allah]." (*Sahih al-Bukhari*, Sulh, 5; *Sahih Muslim*, Aqdiyya, 17, 18. See also: *Sunan ibn Majah*, Muqaddima, 2).

NARRATOR

Aisha

1. Aisha, may Allah be pleased with her, was a very intelligent woman who learned how to read and write at a very young age. She never forgot anything that she had learned and memorized.

2. The most important point in relation to the Prophet's marriage to Aisha, may Allah be pleased with her, was its being contracted through the direct commandment of Allah.

3. The Messenger of Allah, peace and blessings be upon him, loved Aisha, may Allah be pleased with her, greatly. When he was asked, "Who do you love most?" he replied, "Aisha." When he was then asked, "(What about) from among the men?" he said, "Her father."

4. Aisha, may Allah be pleased with her, was born nine years before the Emigration, in the city of Mecca. She passed away on the seventeenth day of Ramadan (676 CE), on a Tuesday, in Medina.

EXPLANATION

An innovation in religion is referred to in Islam as bid'a.

1. Allah declares the following in relevant Qur'anic verses:

$$فَمَاذَا بَعْدَ الْحَقِّ اِلَّا الضَّلَالُ$$

...What is there, after the truth, but error? (Yunus 10:32).

This verse demonstrates that there is no connection between truth and being on the wrong path. What behooves the human being is to be on the side of and in the way of truth. All kinds of innovation in religion and every fabricated thing that does not have its basis in Islam is deviation. Deviation of all kinds has been deemed unacceptable.

$$مَا فَرَّطْنَا فِى الْكِتَابِ مِنْ شَىْءٍ$$

...We have neglected nothing in the Book... (al-An'am 6:38).

Some scholars have asserted that implied in "the Book" is the Qur'an. This is because none of the proofs and obligations necessary for human beings has been omitted therein.

$$فَاِنْ تَنَازَعْتُمْ فِى شَىْءٍ فَرُدُّوهُ اِلَى اللهِ وَالرَّسُولِ$$

...And if you are to dispute among yourselves about anything, refer it to Allah and the Messenger. (an-Nisa 4:59).

Solutions contravening the criteria espoused by Allah and His Messenger and which violate the truths of the Qur'an and the Sunnah lead the human being and society to an impasse. Individuals and even broader society come to believe, at times, that the most perfect solution lies in their self-discovered and tried paths, methods and systems. They can even convince others of this also.

Finding the resolutions to such great issues, however, is only possible through appeal to Allah and His Messenger, and through putting the Qur'an and the Sunnah into practice, without oversight, and freed from any innovations.

This hadith constitutes one of the most important foundations of Islam. Anything that does not rest upon the Book and the Sunnah cannot be accepted. Such a thing cannot be considered to be part of religion.

Those who disregard the worship and deeds befitting the Qur'an and the Sunnah, lessen or alter them and who thus manipulate (corrupt or distort) religion are also innovators in religion. Their deeds too are rejected and are on no account accepted.

Innovation (in religion) is that which does not have a basis in and which cannot be reconciled with the Qur'an or Sunnah and which has no application in the Muslim community. Here, however, it is used to mean the fabrications put forward in religion without an authoritative source.

Rendering inactive the Qur'an and Sunnah or neglecting them breeds innovation and gives rise to their fostering and thriving. In that case, the sole way of preventing innovations in religion is to spread the culture of the Qur'an and Sunnah and to prepare the grounds for these to become a way of life.

That being the case, how must innovations be understood?

According to Imam Shafi'i, innovation is of two kinds: "Anything that contravenes the Qur'an, the Sunnah, the learned consensus, and the way of the Companions is a deviatory and evil innovation; those things and good practices that do not contradict these are good innovations." This is the reason behind the use of the terms *bid'a hasana* (good innovation) and *bid'a sayyi'a* (evil innovation). Shafi'i substantiates this with the words of noble Umar, may Allah be pleased with him, who responded to a group of Companions performing the Tarawih Prayer particular to Ramadan in congregation, remarking, "What a good innovation this is!"

2. The Messenger of Allah, peace and blessings be upon him, said the following in relation to good and evil innovation: "Whoever introduces a good practice that is followed after him, will have the reward for that and the equivalent of their reward, without that detracting from their reward in the slightest. Whoever introduces an evil practice that is followed after him, will bear the burden of sin for that and the equivalent of their burden of

sin, without that detracting from their burden in the slightest." *Sahih Muslim*, Zakah, 69. See also: *Sunan an-Nasa'i*, Zakah, 64.

The Companions undertook a great many things that were not in question during the time of the Prophet, and reached unanimous consensus regarding their acceptance and legitimacy. The Qur'an's being compiled into book form during the caliphate of Abu Bakr, may Allah be pleased with him, and duplicated and distributed to various regions during the caliphate of Uthman, may Allah be pleased with him, are the most known examples in this regard. Efforts in later periods to record, in full, texts of Arabic grammar, the religiously obligatory, accounts, Qur'anic commentary, and hadith constitute further such examples. Even if these are to be termed innovations, they cannot be said to be wrong, as this is precisely how knowledge was preserved, spread and transferred to succeeding generations. This needs to be considered thus with respect to our time and mass media organs, modern printing and publication houses, the Internet, and military and social developments. Those who do not keep pace with such advancements would have no chance of survival in such a world.

3. **The sources of Islamic jurisprudence are clearly defined:**
   a. **The Qur'an:** The leading source in Islamic jurisprudence. The religion of Islam is learned first and foremost from the Qur'an. "The best among you are those who learn the Qur'an and teach it."
   b. **The Sunnah:** The words and actions of the Prophet. Constitutes the second primary source in Islamic jurisprudence. The Sunnah is applied to in the absence of clear injunctions in the Qur'an. In the same way that the Prophet has instructed adherence to his Sunnah, he has also enjoined adherence to the practice of the Four Rightly-Guided Caliphs as well as his Companions. Such innovations as the supererogatory Prayer during Ramadan performed in congregation during the caliphate of Umar, may Allah be pleased with him, and the establishment of the Call to Prayer inside the mosque for the Friday Prayer during Uthman's caliphate, constitute the practice of the Companions and must be followed.

c. **Ijma al-Umma (Consensus of Scholars):** *Ijma* is the term employed to refer to the consensus of Muslim jurists on a theological matter in a given era. The consensus of scholars on a matter is a source of legislation in Islam and is appealed to when a matter is not found in the Qur'an and the Sunnah. For instance, the Tarawih Prayer performed in congregation during Umar's caliphate.

d. **Qiyas al-Fuqaha (Analytical Reasoning of the Scholars):** The term *qiyas* literally means measuring two things with each other and drawing comparisons between them. Umar, may Allah be pleased with him, is known to have advised Abu Musa al-Ash'ari to "Identify similar and analogous cases, carefully examine their causes, and then use *qiyas* (analytical deduction)."

WHAT WE HAVE LEARNED

1. This hadith constitutes one of the cornerstones of Islam. **2.** That which does not abrogate or contradict the Qur'an and Sunnah is accepted (The compilation of the Qur'an in book form, commemoration of the Noble Birth, and the like). **3.** Innovation (*bid'a*) is categorized into good (*hasana*) and evil (*sayyi'a*) innovation. **4.** Muslim scholars have considered innovation in five parts: necessary (*wajib*), recommended (*mandub*), permitted (*mubah*), unlawful (*haram*), and disliked (*makruh*). The discovery of weapons of warfare and the readying of forces suitable for the conditions of the time is necessary. Establishing universities and institutes and publishing scholarly works, spreading knowledge, teaching it to others, building schools and the like are recommended and accepted. Eating and drinking of the lawful is permissible, while the unlawful and disliked have been clearly defined and determined in Islam. **5.** Both the one who sets an evil precedent (in evil innovation) and the one who follows in their path are equally wrongdoers.

EVALUATION

1. What was the distinguishing factor of the Prophet's marriage to Aisha, may Allah be pleased with her?

2. What is *bid'a* and what are its types?

3. What is good and evil innovation according to Imam Shafi'i?
4. What was the Prophet's response to a group of people who said that they would not recognize any source other than the Qur'an?
5. How has the Prophet enjoined following the practices of the Caliphs and Companions?
6. Provide some examples of good innovations in the time of the Caliphs.
7. What are the qualities that Muslim jurists must possess, in general?

UNIT ELEVEN

AMR BIL-MA'RUF WA AN-NAHY AN AL-MUNKAR

(Enjoining the Good and Forbidding the Evil)

عَنْ أَبِي سَعِيدٍ الْخُدْرِيّ قَالَ: سَمِعْتُ رَسُولَ اللهِ صَلَّى اللهُ عَلَيْهِ وَسَلَّمَ يَقُولُ: مَنْ رَأَى مِنْكُمْ مُنْكَرًا فَلْيُغَيِّرْهُ بِيَدِهِ، فَإِنْ لَمْ يَسْتَطِعْ فَبِلِسَانِهِ، فَإِنْ لَمْ يَسْتَطِعْ فَبِقَلْبِهِ وَذٰلِكَ أَضْعَفُ الْإِيمَانِ.

TRANSLATION

Abu Said al-Khudri, may Allah be well pleased with him, said, "I heard the Messenger of Allah, may Allah bless him and grant him peace, say: 'Whoever of you sees something wrong should change it with his hand; if he cannot, then with his tongue; if he cannot, then with his heart, and that is the weakest form of belief.'" (*Sahih Muslim*, Iman, 78. See also: *Sunan at-Tirmidhi*, Fitan, 11; *Sunan an-Nasa'i*, Iman, 17).

NARRATOR

Abu Said al-Khudri

1. Sa'd ibn Malik ibn Sinan ibn Ubayd's father had become Muslim in Medina when the message of Islam was first conveyed in the city; Abu Said was born into a Muslim family. **2.** Abu Said al-Khudri, may Allah be pleased with him, is among the *mukthirun* Companions of the Prophet, who narrated over a thousand hadith. **3.** Abu Said participated in the construction of the Prophet's Mosque in Medina. He was too young to participate in the Battle of Badr, but took part in the Battle of Uhud alongside his father. **4.** He passed away in the seventy-fourth year after the Emigration, at eighty-one years of age.

EXPLANATION

Ma'ruf denotes a thing accepted as good in Islam and encompasses everything in the sphere of obedience to Allah. On the contrary, *Munkar* are those things not approved of in Islam and deemed to be transgression against Allah.

The responsibility of enjoining the *ma'ruf* and forbidding the *munkar* is religiously incumbent upon Muslims. The obligatory nature of this has been established with the Book and the Sunnah. In addition, this religious obligation is one of the greatest of all religious obligations and constitutes the backbone of the religion. The formation of a group that would realize this mission is a collective duty (*fard al-kifaya*). The Muslim community is obligated to raise a community to fulfill this duty. If this is not accomplished, the entire community will be held accountable and cannot be absolved from responsibility.

Allah declares:

اَلْمُنَافِقُونَ وَالْمُنَافِقَاتُ بَعْضُهُمْ مِنْ بَعْضٍ يَأْمُرُونَ بِالْمُنْكَرِ وَيَنْهَوْنَ عَنِ الْمَعْرُوفِ

> The hypocrites, both men and women, are all of a kind: enjoining and promoting what is evil and forbidding and trying to prevent what is right and good... (at-Tawbah 9:67).

However, the qualities of the believers in this regard are described thus:

وَالْمُؤْمِنُونَ وَالْمُؤْمِنَاتُ بَعْضُهُمْ اَوْلِيَاءُ بَعْضٍ يَأْمُرُونَ بِالْمَعْرُوفِ وَيَنْهَوْنَ عَنِ الْمُنْكَرِ

> The believers, both men and women, they are guardians, confidants, and helpers of one another. They enjoin and promote what is right and good and forbid and try to prevent the evil... (at-Tawbah 9:71).

Is the duty of enjoining the good and preventing the evil merely the duty of a community established solely for this task? Don't human beings hold individual responsibilities in this regard?

The obligation of promoting the good and trying to prevent the evil is common to all believers. Such verses as, *"Do you enjoin upon people holiness and virtue but forget your own selves,"* (al-Baqarah 2:44) and *"Most odious it is in the sight of Allah that you say what you do not (and will not) do,*" (as-Saff 61:3) demonstrate that all individuals in society are charged with the duty of enjoining the good and forbidding the evil. No one can absolve themselves in this regard. Advocating the good and striving to prevent the evil to the best of their ability is a command that is absolutely binding on every individual Muslim (*fard al-ayn*).

1. Muslim scholars have asserted that, in the general sense, changing something that is wrong with one's hand is the duty of administrators, changing it with one's tongue is the duty of scholars, and changing it with the heart falls upon the people, and those unable to actualize the others.

If changing an evil is going to give rise to even greater disorder and evil, such as killing, than one must suffice with changing it verbally, or by means of advice and counsel. If speaking is similarly going to endanger or threaten, then trying to change that wrong with one's heart must be preferred. Implied in changing something with one's heart is to view that thing as repugnant and to abhor it inwardly.

2. *Amr bil-ma'ruf wa an-nahy an al-munkar* is a path leading to the purpose of one's creation. Allah revealed for display the palace of the universe for precisely this reason and again charged the human being therein with this mission.

وَلْتَكُنْ مِنْكُمْ أُمَّةٌ يَدْعُونَ اِلَى الْخَيْرِ وَيَأْمُرُونَ بِالْمَعْرُوفِ وَيَنْهَوْنَ عَنِ الْمُنْكَرِ وَاُولَٰئِكَ هُمُ الْمُفْلِحُونَ

> There must be among you a community calling to good, and enjoining and actively promoting what is right, and forbidding and trying to prevent evil (in appropriate ways). They are those who are the prosperous. (Al Imran 3:104).

Indeed, there must be in society, a community carrying out *Amr bilma'ruf wa an-nahy an al-munkar*, inviting to good and prevent wickedness, showing human beings what is true and right, and who are themselves upon the path of righteousness.

If there, is in a particular place, a community enjoining the good and striving to prevent evil, Allah the Almighty promises to protect the people of that place from all afflictions and disasters. It is not possible for another to provide such a guarantee. He declares:

$$ وَمَا كَانَ رَبُّكَ لِيُهْلِكَ الْقُرٰى بِظُلْمٍ وَاَهْلُهَا مُصْلِحُونَ $$

And it has never been the way of your Lord to destroy the townships un-justly while their people were righteous, dedicated to continuous self-re-form and setting things right in the society. (Hud 11:117)

Allah does not impose punishment upon a place wherein the duty of calling people to what is right and working to prevent the wrong is realized. Thus, the Prophet states, "Anyone who creates a good Sunnah in Islam has its reward."

It is not possible to consider the enterprise of promoting good and preventing evil without reflecting upon Mus'ab ibn Umayr, his self-sacrifice, his endeavors, as well as his method:

The First Teacher

The Medinan natives who had embraced Islam at the first Aqaba Allegiance wrote to the Messenger of Allah, peace and blessings be upon him, saying: "O Messenger of Allah, Islam has been declared among us and has begun to spread. Send to us a person who will invite the people to the Book of Allah, to recite the Qur'an to us, teach us the religion of Islam, demonstrate and establish its practices and commandments, and lead us in the Prayer." Upon this, Allah's Messenger, peace and blessings be upon him, appointed Mus'ab ibn Umayr, may Allah be pleased with him, to Medina, instructing him to teach the natives of Medina how to read the Qur'an, to teach them Islam, to help them understand its commandments and prohibitions, and to lead them in Prayer.

Mus'ab ibn Umayr, may Allah be pleased with him, reached Medina in a short time and was greeted with great jubilation. He was hosted at the residence of As'ad ibn Zurara, one of the first Medinan Muslims. There, he began to teach the people their religion and, by virtue of his great efforts and service, Islam spread rapidly throughout the city until it reached every house.

LESSONS FROM THE HADITH

1. The establishment of an administration that would promote the good and work to prevent evil, raising scholars to realize this task, and forming a community to undertake this endeavor is a collective obligation upon the Muslims.
2. Advocating what is right and trying to prevent what is wrong is a duty that is absolutely binding upon every Muslim, to their own ability and capacity.
3. Preventing evil in society with the hand is, broadly speaking, the duty of administrators, prevention with the tongue, or through verbal communication, teaching, counsel and advice, is the duty of scholars and the learned, and reacting to evil with the heart, expressing abhorrence and aversion, is the duty of the community.
4. Promoting the good and trying to prevent the evil is the common responsibility of the Muslim community.

EVALUATION

1. What is the weakest level of belief according to the hadith?
2. How many hadith were narrated by Abu Said al-Khudri? What is his actual name?
3. What is the meaning of *ma'ruf* and *munkar*?
4. "The believers, both men and women, they are guardians, confidants, and helpers of one another. They .... and .... what is right and good and .... and try to .... the evil."

5. "The hypocrites, both men and women, are all of a kind: enjoining and promoting what is ……… and forbidding and trying to prevent what is ……… and ……… ."

6. Changing evil with the hand is the duty of ………, changing these with the tongue is the duty of ………, and reacting with the heart is the duty of ……… .

7. What is the assurance that the residents of a particular place would be protected from affliction and disaster?

8. ……… ends can only be reached through right means.

9. Why did Sufyan al-Thawri refuse going to the presence of Abbasid caliph Harun al-Rashid?

10. What spiritual qualities must a person undertaking *Amr bil-ma'ruf wa an-nahy an al-munkar* possess?

11. What issues needs to be taken into consideration when promoting the good and preventing the evil?

12. Briefly describe Mus'ab ibn Umayr's method of *Amr bil-ma'ruf wa an-nahy an al-munkar*.

13. What does it mean to change a wrong with one's heart?

UNIT TWELVE

SILA AR-RAHM

(Observing Ties of Kinship)

عَنْ أَبِي هُرَيْرَةَ: جَاءَ رَجُلٌ إِلَى رَسُولِ اللهِ صَلَّى اللهُ عَلَيْهِ وَسَلَّمَ فَقَالَ:

يَا رَسُولَ اللهِ مَنْ أَحَقُّ النَّاسِ بِحُسْنِ صَحَابَتِي؟ قَالَ: "أُمَّك" قَالَ: ثُمَّ

مَنْ؟ قَالَ: "أُمَّك" قَالَ: ثُمَّ مَنْ؟ قَالَ: "أُمَّك" قَالَ: ثُمَّ مَنْ؟ قَالَ: أَبُوك.

TRANSLATION

Abu Hurayra, may Allah be pleased with him, said: "A man came to the Messenger of Allah, may Allah bless him and grant him peace, and asked, 'O Messenger of Allah, what person is the most entitled to the best of my company?' He answered, 'Your mother.' He asked, 'Then whom?' He said, 'Your mother.' He asked, 'Then whom?' He said, 'Your mother.' He asked, 'Then whom?' He said, 'Your father.'" (*Sahih al-Bukhari*, Adab, 2; *Sahih Muslim*, Birr, 1. See also: *Sunan ibn Majah*, Wasaya, 4; *Sunan Abu Dawud*, Adab, 120; *Sunan at-Tirmidhi*, Birr, 1).

NARRATOR

Abu Hurayra

1. His name is Abdu'r-Rahman ibn Sakhr. During the Age of Ignorance, his name was Abd ash-Shams (Servant of the Sun). The Messenger of Allah, peace and blessings be upon him, named him Abdu'r-Rahman (and according to other narrations, Abdullah or others). He himself explained why he was given the nickname Abu Hurayra: "I had found a cat and used to carry it with me. For this reason, I came to be known as Abu Hurayra (literally meaning, 'Father of Kitten')." **2.** He became Muslim during the Battle of Khaybar, coming to Medina from Yemen (629 CE). **3.** He was one of the leading figures of the Suffa Companions. **4.** He possessed a strong memory and great intelligence. **5.** He is distinguished among the Companions as having greatest command of and narrating the most hadith. He has narrated 5,374 hadiths. **6.** He is distinguished in hadith narration. **7.** Abu Hurayra, may Allah be pleased with him, passed away in Medina (676 CE), aged seventy-eight years.

EXPLANATION

Allah the Almighty has emphasized kindness to parents and observing the ties of kinship in various sections of the Qur'an and has warned human beings in this regard. Moreover, at times even placing the rights of parents above all else, He has enumerated it immediately after commanding human beings not to associate partners with Him.

وَاعْبُدُوا اللهَ وَلَا تُشْرِكُوا بِهِ شَيْئاً وَبِالْوَالِدَيْنِ اِحْسَاناً وَبِذِى الْقُرْبٰى
وَالْيَتَامٰى وَالْمَسَاكِينِ وَالْجَارِ ذِى الْقُرْبٰى وَالْجَارِ الْجُنُبِ وَالصَّاحِبِ
بِالْجَنْبِ وَابْنِ السَّبِيلِ وَمَا مَلَكَتْ اَيْمَانُكُمْ

And (as the essential basis of contentment in individual, family and social life,) worship Allah and do not associate anything as a partner with Him; and do good to your parents in the best way possible, and to the relatives, orphans, the destitute, the neighbor who is near (in kinship, location, faith), the neighbor who is distant (in kinship and faith), the companion by your side (on the way, in the family, in the workplace, etc.), the wayfarer, and those who are in your service. (an-Nisa 4:36).

يَا اَيُّهَا النَّاسُ اتَّقُوا رَبَّكُمُ الَّذِى خَلَقَكُمْ مِنْ نَفْسٍ وَاحِدَةٍ وَخَلَقَ مِنْهَا
زَوْجَهَا وَبَثَّ مِنْهُمَا رِجَالاً كَثِيراً وَنِسَاءً وَاتَّقُوا اللهَ الَّذِى تَسَاءَلُونَ بِهِ
وَالْاَرْحَامَ اِنَّ اللهَ كَانَ عَلَيْكُمْ رَقِيباً

O humankind! In due reverence for your Lord, keep from disobedience to Him Who created you from a single human self, and from it created its mate, and from the pair of them, scattered abroad a multitude of men and women. In due reverence for Allah, keep from disobedience to Him in Whose name you make demands of one another, and (duly observe) the rights of the wombs (i. e. of kinship, thus observing piety in your rela-

tions with Allah and with human beings). Allah is ever watchful over you
(an-Nisa 4:1)

وَقَضٰى رَبُّكَ اَلَّا تَعْبُدُوا اِلَّا اِيَّاهُ وَبِالْوَالِدَيْنِ اِحْسَاناً اِمَّا يَبْلُغَنَّ عِنْدَكَ
الْكِبَرَ اَحَدُهُمَا اَوْ كِلَاهُمَا فَلَا تَقُلْ لَهُمَا اُفَّ وَلَا تَنْهَرْهُمَا وَقُلْ لَهُمَا
قَوْلاً كَرِيماً ۞ وَاخْفِضْ لَهُمَا جَنَاحَ الذُّلِّ مِنَ الرَّحْمَةِ وَقُلْ رَبِّ
ارْحَمْهُمَا كَمَا رَبَّيَانِى صَغِيراً

Your Lord has decreed that you worship none but Him alone, and treat
parents with the best of kindness. Should one of them, or both, attain old
age in your lifetime, do not say "Ugh!" to them (as an indication of complaint or impatience), nor push them away, and always address them in
gracious words. Lower to them the wing of humility out of mercy, and
say: "My Lord, have mercy on them even as they cared for me in childhood." (al-Isra 17:23-24)

1. Obedience to parents is an important duty to which Allah gives great
weight and which is second only to belief in His Unity, such that He exhorts human beings in this immediately after decreeing that they worship
none but Him. It is inconceivable for those who are not careful in observing the rights of their parents, who have favored them with innumerable
kindness, to duly observe the rights of others. The Messenger of Allah,
peace and blessings be upon him, states that the person most deserving of
the best treatment and conduct is the mother, to such an extent that they
are three times more deserving of such benevolence than the father. This is
because, compared to the father, the mother assumes the three added responsibilities of carrying the child for nine months during pregnancy, giving
birth, and nursing them, among other arduous duties.

2. Again, as reported by Abu Hurayra, may Allah be pleased with him,
the Messenger of Allah, peace and blessings be upon him, said: "What a
loss for him! What a loss for him! What a loss for him!" Someone asked:
'Who, O Allah's Messenger?' He replied: 'He whose parents reach old age,

either one or both of them, but he does not enter Paradise.'" (*Sahih Muslim*, Birr 9, 10).

Notwithstanding the age of their parents, a child is obligated to fulfill their duties towards them. They may be wealthy and not be in need of the financial assistance of their children. They may even have personal carers or employees attending to their daily chores. What falls upon the child in such a circumstance is to please them and to fulfill whatever needs they may have. Money is not everything. An affectionate glance, a heartfelt gesture, and a loving embrace are not things that can be bought with money.

3. Abu Hurayra again reports that Allah's Messenger, peace and blessings be upon him, said: "A child cannot repay his father unless he finds him as a slave and the buys him and sets him free." (*Sahih Muslim*, Itk, 25. See also: *Sunan Abu Dawud*, Adab, 120; *Sunan at-Tirmidhi*, Birr, 8; *Sunan ibn Majah*, Adab, 1).

4. The rights of parents over their children can be categorized as follows:

a) Rights Pertaining to the Body

If need be, we should carry our parents on our back. Upon seeing a man with a burden on his back during his circumambulation of the Ka'ba, Hasan al-Basri asked him why he performed this worship with a burden upon his back. The man replied, "This is not a burden, but is my father. I brought him here from Damascus and circumambulated the Ka'ba seven times with him. He taught me my religion and my belief. He raised me with an Islamic morality; his rights upon me are great." Hasan al-Basri responded, "If you were to carry him on your back until the Last Day, your labor would go to waste in the event of your breaking his heart only once. Similarly, if you please him even once, it would be equivalent to this much labor."

All the favors and spiritual degrees that Uways al-Qarani attained are due to his kindness to his mother. Anas ibn Malik, may Allah be pleased with him, relates: "During the time of Allah's Messenger, there was a young man by the name of Alqama. He was very pious, spending his time in Prayer and fasting. He then fell very ill and, at the subsequent approach of death, became speechless. Being informed of this situation, the Messenger of Allah, peace and blessings be upon him, sent Ali and Ammar ibn Yasir, may Allah be pleased with them, to him. Despite their prompting Alqama to recite the Declaration of Faith, he was unable to do so. When Bilal al-Habashi, may Allah be pleased with him, informed the Prophet of the young man's predicament, Allah's Messenger, peace and blessings be upon him, asked, 'Are either of his parents alive?'

'O Messenger of Allah, his mother is alive, but she is very aged,' he was told.

The Prophet then wished to speak with her. When she arrived, he asked her about her son, and she replied:

'O Messenger of Allah, Alqama is very pious. He is always engaged in worship, but I am displeased with him, as he holds the approval of his wife above mine.'

Allah's Messenger, peace and blessings be upon him, said, 'Your displeasure has prevented Alqama's tongue from pronouncing the Declaration of Faith. Forgive him, so that he may speak.'

When she refused, Allah's Messenger, peace and blessings be upon him, turned to Bilal and said, 'O Bilal, call for my Companions to go out and gather firewood.'

Upon hearing this, she asked, 'O Messenger of Allah, what do you plan to do with this? Will my child be burnt in the fire? How am I to bear this?'

Allah's Messenger, peace and blessings be upon him, said, 'The flames of the Fire are more severe and long-lasting. If you want Allah to forgive him, be reconciled to him. His Prayer, fasting, and spending in charity are of no benefit to Alqama so long as you are displeased with him.'

When the elderly woman heard these words, she exclaimed, 'I call upon Allah and His angels and the Muslims who are present to be my witness that I have forgiven Alqama.'

She then went to her son and heard his voice. He pronounced the Declaration of Faith with ease and passed away that same day. After his burial, Allah's Messenger, peace and blessings be upon him, addressed his Companions saying, 'The curse of Allah and the angels is upon the man who favors his wife over his mother.'"

b) Rights Pertaining to the Tongue

1. We must not even say "Ugh" to our parents. **2.** Not raising one's voice when speaking with them. **3.** Refraining from excessive speech or exceeding the bounds of propriety while in their presence. **4.** Not favoring one's wife over them. **5.** Not calling them by their names or interrupting them as they speak. **6.** Avoiding the use of directives such as "Do" or "Don't", instead asking politely. **7.** Obtaining their blessing.

c) Rights Pertaining to the Heart

1. Having mercy on them, being compassionate towards them. It is stated in a hadith: "Those who show no mercy will be shown no mercy." (*Sahih Muslim*) **2.** Love. One must make one's parents feel loved at all times. Another hadith states: "Kissing the feet of one's mother is like kissing the threshold of the doorway to Paradise." (Shir'a) **3.** Sharing their happiness. One must echo their joy when they are pleased with something. **4.** Sharing their sorrow or pain. If they are upset with something, one must strive to convey one's care and concern. **5.** Being pleased with them. One must seek to attain their pleasure in every possible way.

d) Rights Pertaining to Wealth and Property

1. Preferring one's parents to oneself in dress and eating and drinking. **2.** Visiting them if they are at a distance: "Whoever believes in Allah and the Last Day, let them maintain the bonds of kinship." (*Sahih al-Bukhari*) **3.** Eating together. **4.** Inquiring after their needs and wants and fulfilling these. **5.** Cleaning their homes, undertaking any maintenance required such as painting or other repairs. **6.** Helping them financially. They may be in need of monetary support but may be unable to express this. **7.** Spending freely on them. It is declared in the Qur'an: "*Whatever you spend of your wealth is for (your) parents and the near relatives, and the (needy) orphans, the destitute, and the wayfarer*" (al-Baqarah 2:215). To a person who asked on whom he was to spend, Allah's Messenger, peace and blessings be upon him, said, "Start with your own self and spend it on yourself, and if anything is left, it should be spent on your family, and if anything is left (after meeting the needs of the family) it should be spent on relatives, and if anything is left from the family, it should be spent like this, like this." And he was saying: "In front of you, on your right and on your left." **8.** Inviting them over to share in a meal. This is something that they desire but perhaps cannot articulate. **9.** Being preoccupied with their medical treatment when they fall ill and purchasing their medication. One must strive to care for them themselves instead of hiring a carer to attend to them.

e) Rights after Their Death

1. Making haste with regard to their burial. **2.** Washing them in accordance with the requirements of the Sunnah. One must ensure that the individuals washing them are comprehensively knowledgeable about and skilled in this task. **3.** Shrouding them in accordance with the Prophetic practice. **4.** Obtaining their shroud through their lawful earnings. **5.** Always entreating Allah for their forgiveness. **6.** Personally placing them in the soil. **7.** Performing a helpful service to those who dig the grave and workers at the cemetery. **8.** Burying them among good and righteous people. **9.** Giving in charity by their grave. **10.** Supplicating at their graveside. **11.** Paying their debts. **12.** To recite the *talkin*, or "prompting," at the time of burial, instructing the deceased in the essentials of belief as to how to answer the interrogative angels. It is stated in a hadith: "When one of you dies and you have settled the earth over him, let one of you stand at the head of his grave and then say: 'O So-and-so, son of So-and-so [name of the mother]!' For he will hear him even if he does not reply. Then let him say a second time: 'O So-and-so, son of So-and-so [name of the mother]!' Whereupon he will sit up (in his grave). Then let him say: 'O So-and-so, son of So-and-so [name of the mother]!' At this the deceased will say: 'Instruct me, and may Allah grant you mercy!' Even if you cannot hear it. Then let him say: 'Remember the state in which you left this world, which is your witnessing that there is no deity except Allah, and that Muhammad is His servant and Messenger; that you are pleased with Allah as your Lord, Islam as your religion, Muhammad as your Prophet, and the Qur'an as your book.'" (Daylami) **13.** Carrying out their last will and testament. If their request contravenes the religion, it is not fulfilled. **14.** Entreating Allah in their supplications after the Prayer and conveying the spiritual rewards to their spirits. A hadith states: "If a person is undutiful to their parents but prays for their forgiveness and deliverance after their death, Allah will record them among those dutiful to their parents." (Ibn Abi ad-Dunya) **15.** Fasting on their behalf. It is again stated in hadith: "No one should offer a Prayer or observe a Fast on behalf of another; however, they can feed (the needy) instead." (*Sunan an-Nasa'i*) Someone came to the beloved Prophet and asked, "O Messenger of Allah, my parents have died; is there any act left with which I may be dutiful to them?" Allah's Messenger, peace and blessings be upon him, said, "There are four such things: supplication and asking for their forgiveness, fulfilling their promises, honoring their friends, and maintaining good relations with those of your relatives with whom your kinship is established only through them." (Hakim) **16.** Performing the Pilgrimage and sending them the rewards therein. According to the majority of scholars, undertaking the Pilgrimage on behalf of one's parents is permissible. A hadith states: "Whoever performs the Pilgrimage on behalf of his deceased parents, that Pilgrimage is accepted from both himself and his parents, and the souls of his parents are given the glad tidings of such." (Dar al-Qutni) **17.** Giving in charity on their behalf. As stated in a hadith: "Why should one who gives in charity not convey its reward to the spirit of their deceased parents when both will be rewarded without the reward of the sender not being lessened in the slightest." (Tabarani) **18.** Visiting their graves and reciting the Qur'an: "One who visits the grave of one or both of his parents sincerely with the hope of forgiveness, will receive the reward equivalent to that of a Pilgrimage, and one who visits their graves often, will have angels visiting his grave (after he passes away)." (Hakim) **19.** Visiting their graves on Fridays: "Whoever visits the grave of his parents, both or either of them, every Friday, Allah will forgive all of his sins and include him amongst those who are dutiful to their parents." (*Sunan at-Tirmidhi*) **20.** Honoring their friends. It is stated in a hadith, "The finest act of goodness is that a person should treat kindly the loved ones of his father." (*Sahih Muslim*) **21.** Giving *sadaqa al-fitr* (the compulsory charity paid after the month of Ramadan) in their name, for the rewards to be bestowed upon them. **22.** Offering a sacrifice on their behalf during the Festival of Sacrifice (*Eid al-Adha*). **23.** Preparing their favorite foods and distributing them to the needy and, as such, pleasing their spirits. **24.** Not speaking of their faults: "Speak well of the dead; do not mention their shortcomings." (*Sunan at-Tirmidhi*).

LESSONS FROM THE HADITH

1. One must visit one's parents and relatives, inquire after their welfare and make them happy. **2.** One must assist those who are in difficulty or need. **3.** Ties must never be severed with one's relatives. **4.** One who forsakes their relatives must not forget that they will be deprived of Divine Mercy and compassion. **5.** The person most deserving of goodness and benevolence is the mother. **6.** The person most worthy of honor, goodness, and obedience after the mother is the father.

EVALUATION

1. What is *Sila al-Rahm*?
2. Who is person whom the Prophet declared is worthy of the best of company?
3. What is Abu Hurayra's actual name?
4. Relate one incident demonstrating Abu Hurayra's competence in hadith narration?
5. "Your Lord has decreed that you .... none but Him alone, and treat parents with the best of kindness. Should one of them, or both, attain old age in your lifetime, do not say ".........!" to them, nor push them away, and always address them in .... words."

6. "What a loss for him! What a loss for him! What a loss for him! Whose .... reach old age, either one or both of them, but he does not enter ...."

7. Why was the young Companion Alqama tongue-tied?

8. "Those who show no .... will be .... no mercy."

9. "Kissing the feet of one's .... is like kissing the threshold of the doorway to Paradise."

10. "The finest act of .... is that a person should treat kindly the loved ones of his ...."

UNIT THIRTEEN

MISERLINESS, GENEROSITY AND ALTRUISM

عَنْ أَبِي هُرَيْرَةَ قَالَ: قَالَ رَسُولُ اللهِ صَلَّى اللهُ عَلَيْهِ وَسَلَّمَ: مَا مِنْ يَوْمٍ يُصْبِحُ الْعِبَادُ فِيهِ إِلَّا مَلَكَانِ يَنْزِلَانِ، فَيَقُولُ أَحَدُهُمَا: اَللّٰهُمَّ أَعْطِ مُنْفِقًا خَلَفًا، وَيَقُولُ الْاٰخَرُ: اَللّٰهُمَّ أَعْطِ مُمْسِكًا تَلَفًا.

TRANSLATION

It is related that Abu Hurayra, may Allah be pleased with him, said that the Prophet, may Allah bless him and grant him peace, said: "There is never a day wherein the servants (of Allah) get up in the morning, but are not visited by two angels. One of them says: 'O Allah, give him more who spends (for the sake of Allah)', and the other says: 'O Allah, bring destruction to one who withholds.'" (*Sahih al-Bukhari*, Zakah, 27; *Sahih Muslim*, Zakah, 57).

NARRATOR

Abu Hurayra,[19] may Allah be well pleased with him.

EXPLANATION

1. In the Qur'an, which Allah has sent as the "prescription" for humanity's salvation, Allah places great emphasis on generosity and its benefits. It is declared, for instance:

اَلَّذِينَ يَبْخَلُونَ وَيَأْمُرُونَ النَّاسَ بِالْبُخْلِ وَيَكْتُمُونَ مَا اٰتٰيهُمُ اللهُ مِنْ فَضْلِهِ وَاَعْتَدْنَا لِلْكَافِرِينَ عَذَابًا مُهِينًا

Those who act meanly (in spending out of what Allah has granted them) and urge others to be mean, and conceal the things Allah has granted them out of His bounty (such as wealth or knowledge,

---

[19] Refer to Unit Twelve for further information regarding the narrator Abu Hurayra.

> and certain truths in their Book). We have prepared for (such) un-
> believers a shameful, humiliating punishment. (an-Nisa 4:37)

It can be understood from the verse that Allah has placed meanness among the attributes of unbelievers and has declared that its outcome is a debasing punishment.

As narrated by Adi ibn Hatim, may Allah be pleased with him, the Messenger of Allah, upon him be peace and blessings, said: "So whoever among you can protect himself from the Fire, even with half a date, let him do so."

Spending from the bounties that Allah has favored us with in consideration of His approval and good pleasure is elemental. Allah's Messenger, peace and blessings be upon him, informs us that spending done in this way is among the causes delivering a human being from the Fire.

2. As can be gleaned from the hadith in question, miserliness is also not without is consequence. However, what needs to be pointed out at this juncture is that the wealth that is cursed is the wealth of which the prescribed annual alms are not given. Such destruction and ruin is not asked upon those who are lax with respect to supererogatory goodness.

The word *khalaf* mentioned in the hadith comes to mean that which is given, or received, in place of, or in exchange for, another thing. This takes the form of wealth in this world and rewards in the Hereafter. This is the meaning illustrated in the verse, *"Whatever you spend (in Allah's cause and in alms), He will replace it"* (Saba 34:39). *Talaf* implies physical or immaterial ruin, loss, dissipation, or destruction. It is again declared in a Qur'anic verse: *"Those who spend their wealth night and day, secretly and in public, their reward is with their Lord, and they will have no fear, nor will they grieve"* (al-Baqarah 2:274).

Abu Bakr, may Allah be pleased with him, gave away in charity, at a stroke, the forty thousand dinars in his possession, keeping nothing back—ten thousand at night, ten thousand during the day, ten thousand in secret, ten thousand in public—such that it is said that this verse was revealed in relation to him. When Ali, may Allah be pleased with him, possessed nothing other than four dirhams, he gave away all of these, one by night, one by day, the third secretly and the fourth openly. When the Prophet asked him why he had done so, he replied, "In order to be merit my Lord's words." Upon this, Allah's Messenger, peace and blessings be upon him, affirmed that he had.

3. Again, with respect to altruism, the highest level of generosity, it has been stated: *"And (indeed) they prefer them over themselves, even though poverty be their own lot"* (al-Hashr 59:9).

As is evident in the verse above, altruism refers to preferring the needs of another to one's own needs, even if one is in more need themselves.

4. Allah's Messenger, peace and blessings be upon him, was the most generous of people. He himself stated:

"The generous are near to Allah, near to Paradise, and near to people, and distant from Hell. The miserly, however, are distant from Allah, distant from Paradise, and distant from human beings, but near to Hell." The best of humankind in terms of his life and outward appearance (*ahsan an-nas*), the Prophet was the most generous of people (*ajwad an-nas*) in heart and giving to others.

A great many hearts unable to be unlocked with the keys of tenderness and other lofty feelings were opened to him with the key of generosity. Safwan ibn Umayya was one of these: "Anas reports that when the Messenger of Allah was on his way to Hunayn, he had borrowed some weapons from Safwan ibn Umayya. As Allah's Messenger, peace and blessings be upon him, inspected the war spoils he noticed Safwan gazing upon the herds that were crowding around him in bewilderment and said that Safwan could have as many camels as he wanted. Allah's Messenger, peace and blessings be upon him, continued giving to Safwan until Safwan was astounded by such generosity. With a heart that was filled with abhorrence of the Prophet, Safwan had changed at once. Indeed, this generosity caused Safwan to abandon his hatred and Allah's Messenger, peace and blessings be upon him, thus became the dearest of people to him. Winning over Safwan's heart was of course more precious than thousands of camels and cattle. This generosity shown towards him was not in vain. Safwan immediately ran to his people and announced: 'O my people! Accept Islam without hesitation, for Muhammad gives in such a way that only one who has no fear of poverty and relies fully on Allah can give!' Such generosity was enough to guide Safwan and his people, who had been among the bitterest enemies of Islam until just before that day, to the truth."

ALLAH GIVES TEN FOR ONE

A beggar wanted something from Ali, may Allah be pleased with him. The latter then instructed one of his sons, Hasan or Husayn, saying, "Go to your mother and bring one of the six dirhams that I gave to her." Upon his return, his son said, "My mother said that she is withholding these to buy flour." Ali then replied, "A person cannot be said to have truly believed until they trust in Allah more than they trust in whatever they have. Go and bring all of that money." Fatima subsequently sent the money in its entirety. Ali then gave all of it to the beggar.

Scarcely a few minutes had passed when a camel trader arrived. Upon learning that the camel trader was selling the camel for one hundred and forty dirhams, Ali asked if he could purchase the animal on credit. The seller agreed, tethered his camel there and left.

A short while later, another man arrived and offered to buy the camel from Ali for two hundred dirhams. After paying his creditor the one hundred and forty dirhams, Ali, may Allah be pleased with him, went home and gave his wife Fatima, may Allah be pleased with her, the balance of sixty dirhams, from whom he had only earlier taken six dirhams. When she inquired in astonishment as to what these were for, Ali, may Allah be pleased with him, replied, "It is the result of Allah's promise, through Allah's Messenger, '*Whoever comes to Allah with a good deed will have ten times as much*'" (al-An'am 6:160).

LESSONS FROM THE HADITH

1. Good is never left unrewarded. 2. Close-fistedness and sullenness is to no avail. 3. The wealth of the well to do, who do not pay their prescribed annual alms despite their affluence, is deserving of ruin and destruction. 4. The angels too entreat Allah. That their supplication is answered is demonstrated in the hadith, "When one of you says, *Amin*, as do the angels in the heaven, and they coincide with one another, he will be forgiven his past sins." (*Sahih al-Bukhari*, Ba'd al-Khalq, 7).

EVALUATION

1. "How do the two angels visiting a person each morning entreat Allah?"
2. Protect yourself from the Fire, even with half a ……….
3. What is implied in the terms *khalaf* and *talaf* used in the hadith?
4. What is altruism? Provide an example.
5. From which of Allah's Names is generosity derived?
6. Provide an example of the Prophet's generosity.

UNIT FOURTEEN

PRIDE AND HUMILITY

عَنْ عَبْدِ اللهِ بْنِ مَسْعُودٍ عَنِ النَّبِيِّ صَلَّى اللهُ عَلَيْهِ وَسَلَّمَ قَالَ: "لَا يَدْخُلُ الْجَنَّةَ مَنْ كَانَ فِي قَلْبِهِ مِثْقَالُ ذَرَّةٍ مِنْ كِبْرٍ"، فَقَالَ رَجُلٌ: إِنَّ الرَّجُلَ يُحِبُّ أَنْ يَكُونَ ثَوْبُهُ حَسَنًا وَنَعْلُهُ حَسَنَةً ،قَالَ: "إِنَّ اللهَ جَمِيلٌ يُحِبُّ الْجَمَالَ، اَلْكِبْرُ بَطَرُ الْحَقِّ وَغَمْطُ النَّاسِ".

TRANSLATION

Abdullah ibn Mas'ud, may Allah be well pleased with him, reported that the Prophet, may Allah bless him and grant him peace, said: "No one who has an atom's weight of pride in his heart will enter Paradise."

A man said, "And if the man likes his clothes to be good and his sandals to be good?" Allah's Messenger, peace and blessings be upon him, said: "Allah is Beautiful and loves beauty. Pride means to renounce the truth and abase people." (*Sahih Muslim*, Iman, 147. See also: *Sunan Abu Dawud*, Libas, 26; *Sunan at-Tirmidhi*, Birr, 61).

NARRATOR

Abdullah ibn Mas'ud

1. One of the leading Companions, Abdullah ibn Mas'ud, may Allah be pleased with him, is among the first of those to believe. **2.** He is the first Companion to openly recite the Qur'an in Mecca. **3.** Abdullah ibn Mas'ud is the Companion who killed Abu Jahl. **4.** He was a gifted reciter of the Qur'an. **5.** Ibn Mas'ud is one of the founders of Islamic jurisprudence, being of the Companions well versed in the religion. He is, in particular, the linchpin of the Hanafi school of jurisprudence. **6.** He returned to Medina towards the end of Uthman's caliphate. Falling ill at age sixty, he passed away in the thirty-second year after the Emigration.

EXPLANATION

1. Pride refers to haughty self-conceit and refusal to submit to Allah. The Almighty has cautioned human beings in this regard throughout the Qur'an: "...*Allah does not love those who are conceited and boastful*" (an-Nisa 4:36).

اِنَّ الْمُبَذِّرِينَ كَانُوا اِخْوَانَ الشَّيَاطِينِ وَكَانَ الشَّيْطَانُ لِرَبِّهِ كَفُوراً

Do not strut about the earth in haughty self-conceit; for you can never split the earth (no matter how hard you stamp your foot), nor can you stretch to the mountains in height (no matter how strenuously you seek to impress). (al-Isra 17:37).

While these verses exhort human beings to be mindful of pride and arrogance, another again describes the human attribute of pride as being in actual fact a Satanic attribute and explains that unnecessary pride constitutes an obstacle to submission to the Divine command. For even Satan was banished from Paradise due to his pride:

قَالَ يَا اِبْلِيسُ مَا مَنَعَكَ اَنْ تَسْجُدَ لِمَا خَلَقْتُ بِيَدَيَّ اَسْتَكْبَرْتَ اَمْ كُنْتَ

مِنَ الْعَالِينَ

(Allah) said: "O Iblis! What prevents you from prostrating before the being whom I have created with My two Hands? Are you too proud (to bow down before any created being in defiance of My command), or are you (of those who think themselves) so high in honor (that they cannot be ordered to prostrate before anyone)?" (Saad 38:75).

2. While Allah warns human beings in relation to pride and self-conceit, He has employed verses of encouragement concerning its exact opposite, modesty and humility, even characterizing such people as "the (true) servants of the All-Merciful":

وَعِبَادُ الرَّحْمٰنِ الَّذِينَ يَمْشُونَ عَلَى الْأَرْضِ هَوْناً وَاِذَا خَاطَبَهُمُ الْجَاهِلُونَ قَالُوا سَلَاماً

The (true) servants of the All-Merciful are they who move on the earth gently and humbly, and when the ignorant, foolish ones address them (with insolence or vulgarity as befits their ignorance and foolishness), they response with (words of) peace, (without engaging in hostility with them). (al-Furqan 25:63).

From this standpoint, those who are proud and obstinate enough in their pride not to prostrate before Allah assume the characteristic not of being the servants of the All-Merciful, but on the contrary, being servants of Satan.

3. The hadith under consideration indicates that a person with even the most minuscule amount of pride in their heart will not enter Paradise.

A conceited person will either face punishment until they are completely cleansed of this affliction and then enter Paradise as a result of their belief, or Allah, Who has full power over everything, will forgive that servant and place them in His Paradise with a heart that is purified.

We learn also that the desire to dress well is not connected with pride. What can be the wisdom behind a seemingly wicked characteristic being placed in the nature of a human being?

This quality has been given to the human being with a view to their protecting the position of Islam, the honor of the Qur'an, religion, their spiritual values, their integrity, and similar cherished things. If a person is to have pride, they ought to have it in protecting these. Unfortunately in our day, however, people have for some reason become rather lax and lazy in protecting these; but they have become quite industrious and even oversensitive when it comes to their personal pride. The Pharaohs, Nimrods, and the Abu Lahabs have lost because of their pride.

4. After all, does Allah not charge His Messenger with humility, through the language of the Qur'an: "*Spread your wings (to provide care and shelter) over the believers who follow you (in practicing Allah's com-*

mandments in their lives)" (ash-Shu'ara 26:215). There are many such verses in the Qur'an.

Moreover, Allah's Messenger, peace and blessings be upon him, sought the same thing, wanting to be "a Prophet slave" when Allah had asked him. This is why we say, "Muhammad is His servant and His Messenger," in the Declaration of Faith.

5. Acknowledging all the bounties that Allah has bestowed is a form of thankfulness. This, in turn, leads to an increase in such bounties. Turning a blind eye to Him, however, is ingratitude; ingratitude necessitates punishment and causes the discontinuance of the bounty. A person must always see everything as coming from Allah and must proclaim, "Everything is from You, and You are the All-Wealthy. To You have I turned my face."

However, a person must not conceal the Divinely bestowed bounties in fear of being arrogant. That is, a person must also know how to announce and testify to Allah's favors when necessary. So, how is this balance to be maintained?

As a case in point, a man gives a coat to someone as a gift. If another man says to the bearer of the gift, who is wearing the coat, "How fine you are," and he responds by saying, "The beauty is in the coat," then he would have combined humility with verbal expression and announcement of the bounty.

WHAT WE HAVE LEARNED

1. If pride has reached the point of disrespect towards Allah, the proud person forfeits the chance of entry into Paradise. **2.** People who see themselves as superior to others and are thus haughty and conceited commit a major sin. **3.** A person can dress finely, provided that they are not overtaken by arrogance and self-conceit. **4.** A person must see their own shortcomings if they wish to free themselves of pride and arrogance. A person who does not see their own faults cannot achieve self-correction.

EVALUATION

1. "Allah is ……… and loves ………. . Pride means to renounce the truth and abase people."

2. Who is the Companion who was the first to publicly recite the Qur'an in Mecca and who killed Abu Jahl?

3. "The (true) servants of the All-Merciful are they who move on the earth ……… and ………, and when the ignorant, foolish ones address them, they response with (words of) ……… ."

4. What is the wisdom behind an outwardly evil character trait such as pride being placed in human nature?

5. What does it mean to announce and testify to Allah's Blessings and how is this realized?

6. How does Satan deceive a person by means of pride?

UNIT FIFTEEN

PROPRIETY AND MODESTY

عَنْ عِمْرَانَ بْنِ حُصَيْنٍ رَضِيَ اللهُ عنه أَنَّ النَّبِيَّ صَلَّى اللهُ عَلَيْهِ
وَسَلَّمَ قَالَ: "الْحَيَاءُ لَا يَأْتِي إِلَّا بِخَيْرٍ".

TRANSLATION

As reported by Imran ibn Husayn, may Allah be pleased with him, the Messenger of Allah, may Allah bless him and grant him peace, said: "Modesty only brings good." (*Sahih al-Bukhari*, Adab, 77; *Sahih Muslim*, Iman, 60).

NARRATOR

Imran ibn Husayn

1. Imran ibn Husayn, may Allah be pleased with him, embraced Islam in the year 628, during the conquest of Khaybar. He served as standard-bearer of the Khuda'a tribe during Mecca's conquest. **2.** He was appointed by Umar, may Allah be pleased with him, to teach the people of Basra Islam, at the city's establishment. Later, upon the request of Governor of Basra appointed by Caliph Uthman, may Allah be pleased with him, Ziyad ibn Abi Sufyan, he was appointed to the position of chief judge of Basra. After retiring from office, he spent the remainder of his life teaching hadith in Basra's mosque. **3.** He passed away in Basra in the year 672.

EXPLANATION

Modesty (*haya*) or a sense of shame, like belief, prevents a person from committing evil and deters them from wrongdoing. Thus, modesty only brings good to a human being and it quickly becomes evident that it is altogether good. That is to say, irrespective of its source, a sense of modesty only brings goodness for the human being, from beginning to end.

Unfortunately, there is an attempt in our day to debilitate this elevated feeling. Those who make an effort to show immodesty as a requirement of modernity and who dismiss it as nonsense, perpetrate the greatest evil against the human being. By corrupting their sense of shame and responsibility, they inhibit a person's endeavor to perfect themselves.

1. Allah has cautioned both Muslim women and Muslim men separately concerning modesty and has openly revealed the manner in which they are to act in this regard:

$$قُلْ لِلْمُؤْمِنِينَ يَغُضُّوا مِنْ اَبْصَارِهِمْ وَيَحْفَظُوا فُرُوجَهُمْ ذٰلِكَ اَزْكَى لَهُمْ$$

$$اِنَّ اللهَ خَبِيرٌ بِمَا يَصْنَعُونَ$$

Tell the believing men that they should restrain their gaze (from looking at the women whom it is lawful for them to marry, and from others' private parts), and guard their private parts and chastity. This is what is purer for them. Allah is fully aware of all that they do. (an-Nur 24:30)

While this verse addresses believing men specifically, the verse below is directed at believing women:

$$وَقُلْ لِلْمُؤْمِنَاتِ يَغْضُضْنَ مِنْ اَبْصَارِهِنَّ وَيَحْفَظْنَ فُرُوجَهُنَّ وَلَا يُبْدِينَ$$

$$زِينَتَهُنَّ اِلَّا مَا ظَهَرَ مِنْهَا$$

And tell the believing women that they (also) should restrain their gaze (from looking at the men whom it is lawful for them to marry, and from others' private parts), and guard their private parts, and that they should not display their charms except that which is revealed of itself. (an-Nur 24:31)

Literally meaning reserve and shame, *haya* in the Islamic sense refers to fear of Allah, refraining from saying or doing anything improper or indecent, to describe one who, out of fear and awe of Allah, seeks to avoid displeasing Him.

Indeed, every human being has an innate, Divinely bestowed sense of modesty. However, when this instinctive feeling of modesty is nourished and developed with the modesty at the essence of the religion of Islam, it forms the greatest safeguard against shameful or indecent acts. Alone, and under specific circumstances, it may be diminished or even utterly lost.

If this innate feeling of shame is not combined with awareness coming from belief and expressed in verses like: "*Does he (who would impede the servant in his Prayer) not know that Allah sees (all that people do)?*" (al-Alaq 96:14) and consciousness of Allah's constant oversight: "*Allah is ever watchful over you*" (an-Nisa 4:1), it cannot last long, for both its existence and its continuation depends on belief.

The modesty of every human being changes in accordance with their degree of belief. Needless to say, just as Prophets are examples in every other regard, they are examples for humankind with respect to modesty also.

Despite his body being afflicted with uncountable wounds and illnesses for years on end, Prophet Ayyub (Job), peace be upon him, out of his modesty, did not entreat Allah to heal him, but instead was content with presenting his situation to his Lord and called out to Him, saying: "*Truly, affliction has visited me (so that I can no longer worship You as I must); and You are the Most Merciful of the merciful*" (al-Anbiya 21:83).

When, according to one narration, Allah's Messenger, peace and blessings be upon him, was at Al-Aqsa Mosque during the Ascension, and Archangel Jabrail asked him, "O Allah's Messenger, ask the spirits of all the Prophets if there is any deity worthy of worship other than Allah," the Prophet replied, "I will not ask them, because I have no doubt (as to the answer)." He thus demonstrated exactly what true belief and modesty entails.

LESSONS FROM THE HADITH

1. *Haya*, or a sense of shame, deters a person from the vile or shameful acts unbecoming to the character of a believer. **2.** Belief distances a person from indecency and wrongdoing. **3.** Modesty contributes to an increase and resultant perfection of belief.

EVALUATION

1. What is the literal and contextual meaning of *haya*?
2. How many kinds of modesty are there? What are these?
3. Why did Allah place in Paradise an old man, whose hair and beard had grown white, despite his denial of his sin?
4. "Allah the Almighty feels ashamed to punish those of my Community whose ……… have turned ………, but those of my Community with white beards do not feel ……… to commit ……… ."
5. Describe the modesty of Prophet Yusuf (Joseph).
6. Provide a description of Prophet Muhammad's modesty.

UNIT SIXTEEN

THE TONGUE

عَعَنْ عَبْدِ اللهِ بْنِ عَمْرِو بْنِ الْعَاصِ عَنِ النَّبِيِّ صَلَّى اللهُ عَلَيْهِ
وَسَلَّمَ قَالَ: اَلْمُسْلِمُ مَنْ سَلِمَ الْمُسْلِمُونَ مِنْ لِسَانِهِ وَيَدِهِ،
وَالْمُهَاجِرُ مَنْ هَجَرَ مَا نَهَى اللهُ عَنْهُ.

TRANSLATION

It was related from Abdullah ibn Amr, may Allah be pleased with him, that the Prophet, may Allah bless him and grant him peace, said: "A Muslim is the one from whose tongue and hand the Muslims are safe. An emigrant (*muhajir*) is someone who abandons what Allah has forbidden." (*Sahih al-Bukhari*, Iman 4, 5 Riqaq, 26; *Sahih Muslim*, Iman, 64–65. See also: *Sunan Abu Dawud*, Jihad, 2; *Sunan at-Tirmidhi*, Qiyama, 52, Iman, 12, *Sunan an-Nasa'i*, Iman 8, 9, 11).

NARRATOR

Abdullah ibn Amr ibn al-As

1. Abdullah ibn Amr ibn al-As was the son of Amr ibn al-As, may Allah be pleased with them. **2.** Due to his exceptional generosity and open-handedness, he used to distribute everything that he acquired and thus made everyone happy. **3.** The most significant battle that Abdullah ibn Amr participated in following the Age of Happiness was Yarmuk. **4.** He passed away at seventy-five years of age (684 CE) in Fustat, Egypt, where he was buried.

EXPLANATION

1. In this hadith, Allah's Messenger, peace and blessings be upon him, describes the Muslim as one who does not harm others. Being a person from whose tongue and hand all Muslim men and women, and according to another narration all other people, are safe and

secure, is not as easy as it is supposed. A person cannot be of benefit and do good all the time, but it is possible for no harm to come from them.

The fact that the tongue is mentioned before the hand in the text of the hadith is due to the harm caused with the tongue, such as insult, backbiting, slander, and rumor, being comparably easier, more common and irreparable. Harming others with one's hand or physically persecuting others is not that simple. That a person who holds their tongue is saved (*Sunan at-Tirmidhi*, Qiyama, 50), and those who believe in Allah and the Last Day must speak good or keep silent (*Sahih al-Bukhari*, Adab, 31) are again among the Prophetic counsel.

The hadith under consideration presents the emigrant as a person who steers well clear of what Allah has prohibited. This tradition, on the one hand, points out that it is possible to emigrate at all times and places; on the other hand, it illustrates that a person who takes pains not to harm others and adheres to the command in this regard has attained the status of the true emigrant in this sense.

2. In many verses of the Qur'an, the Almighty has stressed the need for being soft-spoken and gentle in speech.

$$وَاِمَّا تُعْرِضَنَّ عَنْهُمُ ابْتِغَاءَ رَحْمَةٍ مِنْ رَبِّكَ تَرْجُوهَا فَقُلْ لَهُمْ قَوْلاً مَيْسُوراً$$

But if you (must) turn away from those (who are in need, because you are yourself in need, and) seeking mercy from your Lord in hopeful expectation, then (at least) speak to them gently and well-meaning. (al-Isra 17:28)

A true Muslim is a person who inspires complete trust and confidence, so much so that all other Muslims can rely on them without a second thought.

3. In another hadith related by Imam Bukhari in his *Sahih*, Allah's Messenger, peace and blessings be upon him, says, "Whoever can guarantee (the chastity of) what is between his two jaw-bones and what

is between his two legs (i.e. his tongue and his private parts), I guarantee Paradise for him."

4. Speaking little: Excessive speech neither makes one more eloquent nor increases their influence. On the contrary, one's purpose needs to be explained in a manner that is clear, concise, and intelligible. Just as there is no need to leave unsaid what needs to be said in order to be eloquent in speech, there is also no sense in straining others' patience and wearing them by being repetitive or tedious with unnecessary information.

5. Silence is a very important characteristic. Speaking little indicates good conduct. The tongue's talking about Allah is better than empty talk and affords tranquility and repose to the heart.

If speech is silver, silence is gold. Holding one's tongue when it is necessary to remain silent is elemental. The most perfect being in the universe has not been created to be preoccupied with futile and useless things.

LESSONS FROM THE HADITH

1. A Muslim is a trustworthy person. **2.** A good Muslim is a person from whose tongue and hand all other Muslims are safe and secure. **3.** Disturbing, harassing or offending Muslims either verbally or physically has been prohibited. One needs to adhere to this prohibition if they are to be a good Muslim. **4.** The true emigrants are those who abandon what Allah has forbidden.

EVALUATION

1. "A Muslim is the one from whose ……… and ……… the Muslims are safe. An emigrant (*muhajir*) is someone who abandons what Allah has ……… ."

2. What was the most important battle in which Abdullah ibn Amr participated after the Age of Happiness?

3. What has the Prophet said that those who believe in Allah and Last Day must do?

4. Through the guarantee of which two organs has the Prophet guaranteed Paradise?

5. In what manner has Allah enjoined that calling people to His way must be realized?

6. To what does Allah's Messenger, peace and blessings be upon him, liken an assembly, which disperses without Allah's Name having been invoked therein?

7. A person must always speak the ...., but it is not right to speak every .... everywhere.

UNIT SEVENTEEN

BACKBITING, SLANDER

عَنْ أَنَسٍ رَضِيَ اللهُ عنه قَالَ: قَالَ رَسُولُ اللهِ صَلَّى اللهُ عَلَيْهِ وَسَلَّمَ:
لَمَّا عُرِجَ بِي مَرَرْتُ بِقَوْمٍ لَهُمْ أَظْفَارٌ مِنْ نُحَاسٍ يَخْمِشُونَ وُجُوهَهُمْ
وَصُدُورَهُمْ، فَقُلْتُ: مَنْ هَؤُلَاءِ يَا جِبْرِيلُ؟ قَالَ: هَؤُلَاءِ الَّذِينَ
يَأْكُلُونَ لُحُومَ النَّاسِ وَيَقَعُونَ فِي أَعْرَاضِهِمْ

TRANSLATION

Anas ibn Malik, may Allah be pleased with him, reported that the Messenger of Allah, may Allah bless him and grant him peace, said: "When I ascended through the heavens, I passed by some people holding copper nails with which they were gouging their faces and chests.

I said, 'Who are these, Jibril?'

He said, 'Those are the people who consumed people's flesh and attacked their honor.'" (*Sunan Abu Dawud*, Adab, 35).

NARRATOR

Anas ibn Malik

1. Anas ibn Malik, may Allah be pleased with him, was born in Mecca in the year 613 and passed away in Basra, in 709 (90 AH). **2.** When the Messenger of Allah, peace and blessings be upon him, emigrated to Medina, Anas ibn Malik was only ten years old. **3.** After the Prophet's arrival in Medina, Anas ibn Malik's mother held her son by the hand and took him to the presence of Allah's Messenger, peace and blessings be upon him, and said, "O Messenger of Allah, I have raised my child in great hardship. I have nothing (else) with which to help you. This is my son, Anas. I entrust him to your care and for your service. Please let him serve you." The Messenger of Allah, peace and blessings be upon him, could not turn down this earnest request and took Anas ibn Malik under his care. He kept Anas by his side at all times. **4.** Despite being just twelve years of age at the Battle of Badr, Anas went to the battlefield to serve the Muslim troops during the battle and did not neglect his service of Allah's Messenger, peace and blessings be upon him. **5.** Remaining in Medina during Umar's caliphate, Anas ibn Malik spent most of his time teaching Muslim canonical jurisprudence. He passed away at around eighty years of age in Baghdad. **6.** Entreating Allah for Anas, the Prophet had said, "O Allah, increase him in wealth and offspring, and accept him into Paradise."

EXPLANATION

Backbiting is speaking of someone, in their absence and without their knowledge, in way with which they would be displeased or offended. Allah's Messenger, peace and blessings be upon him, said, "Do you know what backbiting is?" They (the Companions) said, "Allah and His Messenger know best." He said, "To mention your brother in a manner he dislikes." It was said, "What if my brother is as I say?" He said, "If he is as you said, you have backbitten him. If he is not as you said, you have slandered him." This hadith is reported in *Sahih Muslim*, *Sunan Abu Dawud*, *Sunan at-Tirmidhi*, *Sunan at-Nasa'i*, as well as others.

1. On account of all people being brothers and sisters in Islam and due to the community of Prophet Muhammad, peace and blessings be upon him, all being like the different members of the one family, the believers do not plot against one another, like the hypocrites, and refrain from any action or behavior that causes harm to their fellow believer. For this reason, Allah has declared all believers brothers and sisters and has likened backbiting to a repugnant savagery as eating the flesh of one's believing brother or sister:

يَا اَيُّهَا الَّذِينَ اٰمَنُوا اجْتَنِبُوا كَثِيراً مِنَ الظَّنِّ اِنَّ بَعْضَ الظَّنِّ اِثْمٌ وَلَا تَجَسَّسُوا وَلَا يَغْتَبْ بَعْضُكُمْ بَعْضاً اَيُحِبُّ اَحَدُكُمْ اَنْ يَأْكُلَ لَحْمَ اَخِيهِ مَيْتاً فَكَرِهْتُمُوهُ وَاتَّقُوا اللّهَ اِنَّ اللّهَ تَوَّابٌ رَحِيمٌ

> O you who believe! Avoid much suspicion, for some suspicion is a grave sin (liable to Allah's punishment); and do not spy (on one another), nor back- bite (against one another). Would any of you love to eat the flesh of his dead brother? You would abhor it! Keep from disobedience to Allah in reverence for Him and piety. Surely Allah is One Who truly returns repentance with liberal forgiveness and additional reward, All-Compassionate (particularly towards His believing servants). (al-Hujurat 49:12)

The expression, "Would any of you love to eat the flesh of his dead brother?" describes the inherent evil and vileness of backbiting. Due to the absence of person who is spoken ill of, their ignorance of what is being said and their resultant inability to defend themselves at that very moment, they are consequently like the dead and are therefore a dead sister or brother. Launching an attack on their honor, in such a situation, by speaking ill of them is vividly depicted in the verse as a brutality and savagery akin to pulling to pieces the flesh of a dead person and then consuming it.

2. Allah declares: *"O you who believe! Avoid much suspicion, for some suspicion is a grave sin (liable to Allah's punishment)…"* (al-Hujurat 49:12).

3. Backbiting is a base weapon used by those who harbor enmity, jealousy, and obstinacy in their heart. An honorable and valiant person does not stoop to using such a vile weapon.

THE REMEDY FOR BACKBITING

This remedy is of two kinds:

1. Through knowledge. This is also divided into two categories:

    a. To contemplate the Prophetic Traditions concerning backbiting and reflect upon and be very aware of its adverse repercussions.

    b. A person must consider his or her own shortcomings and failings that can be backbitten. If they see a flaw within themselves, they must not accuse one who backbites them.

2. To bear in mind the causes driving them to backbite others. There are four such causes:

First Cause: Being angry or resentful, for a particular reason, of the person one backbites. The Prophet says, "Whoever suppresses his rage, while he is able to exact it, Allah will bring him forward before all of creation [on the Day of Judgment] so that he can choose whichever of the heavenly servants he wishes."

Second Cause: A person who backbites follows suit with others so as to earn their approval. The remedy for this is as follows: as seeking the approval of the people leads to Divine wrath and punishment, one must forever seek Allah's good pleasure and approval.

Third Cause: People desire self-praise, but are unable to openly praise themselves; thus, they backbite others so that their superiority can be revealed.

Fourth Cause: Envy and jealousy.

WHAT WE HAVE LEARNED

1. Those who backbite and who presume to toy with the honor and dignity of others will be sentenced to the punishment of scratching their faces and necks with nails made of copper in the Hereafter.
2. Backbiting is a most vile and base weapon injurious to the love and respect between people.
3. The sin of backbiting is among those sins which entail violations of the rights of others. Divine forgiveness may not be possible without having obtained the pardon of the person backbitten against.

EVALUATION

1. According to the hadith, what was the wrongdoing that those scraping their skin with copper nails committed in the world?
2. What is the difference between backbiting and slander?
3. For whom did the Prophet entreat Allah, saying, "O Allah, increase him in wealth and offspring, and accept him into Paradise"?
4. To what brutal and abhorrent act does Allah liken backbiting?
5. In what circumstances may backbiting be permissible?
6. What are the causes of backbiting?

UNIT EIGHTEEN

MUSLIM FELLOWSHIP

عَنِ ابْنِ عُمَرَ رَضِيَ اللهُ عَنْهما أَنَّ رَسُولَ اللهِ صَلَّى اللهُ عَلَيْهِ وَسَلَّمَ قَالَ:
"اَلْمُسْلِمُ أَخُو الْمُسْلِمِ لَا يَظْلِمُهُ وَلَا يُسْلِمُهُ، مَنْ كَانَ فِي حَاجَةِ أَخِيهِ
كَانَ اللهُ فِي حَاجَتِهِ، وَمَنْ فَرَّجَ عَنْ مُسْلِمٍ كُرْبَةً فَرَّجَ اللهُ عَنْهُ بِهَا كُرْبَةً
مِنْ كُرَبِ يَوْمِ الْقِيَامَةِ، وَمَنْ سَتَرَ مُسْلِمًا سَتَرَهُ اللهُ يَوْمَ الْقِيَامَةِ"

TRANSLATION

Ibn Umar, may Allah be pleased with him, reported that the Messenger of Allah, may Allah bless him and grant him peace, said: "A Muslim is the brother of another Muslim. He should not wrong him nor surrender him to his enemy. Allah will take care of the needs of anyone who takes care of the needs of his brother. On the Day of Judgment, Allah will dispel the anxiety of anyone who dispels the anxiety of another Muslim. On the Day of Judgment Allah will veil anyone who veils another Muslim." (*Sahih al-Bukhari*, Mazalim, 3; *Sahih Muslim*, Birr, 58).

NARRATOR

Abdullah ibn Umar

1. It is reported that Abdullah ibn Umar, may Allah be pleased with him, was born in the third year of Prophethood. **2.** He embraced Islam at a young age, along with his father, and emigrated to Medina again with his father. **3.** He was raised entirely in the Muslim community and with an Islamic training and education. **4.** He participated in all battles alongside Allah's Messenger, peace and blessings be upon him, from age eighteen onwards. **5.** He passed away in 74 AH, aged 84, 85, or 86.

EXPLANATION

1. This hadith, first and foremost, declares Muslims brothers and sisters, precisely as is declared in the tenth verse of the Qur'anic chapter

Al-Hujurat. This fellowship has been Divinely determined and is a powerful fellowship encompassing both this world and the Hereafter. For instance, if the brother or sister of a Muslim has lost a loved one, they must attend their funeral and offer their condolences. The Muslim must visit their brother or sister if they are ill, give them morale and attend to any of their needs. It is reported in one hadith that Allah will say on the Day of Judgment: "O son of Adam, I fell ill and you visited Me not." He will say: "O Lord, and how should I visit You when You are the Lord of the worlds?" He will say: "Did you not know that My servant So-and-so had fallen ill and you visited him not? Did you not know that had you visited him you would have found Me with him?" Just as there is a great deal that falls upon the believer—such as responding to the greeting of their fellow Muslim, entreating Allah for their forgiveness, for instance saying "May Allah have mercy on you" when they sneeze, counseling them when they request advice—the virtue of desiring for their fellow believer what they desire for themselves is also expected of them. And this is only possible through true love, such that Allah's Messenger, peace and blessings be upon him, stresses its importance saying, "By the one who has my soul in His hand, you will not enter Paradise until you believe, and you will not believe until you love one another."

2. The second point that is demonstrated in the hadith is that a Muslim does not wrong their fellow believer. In other words, they do not violate any of their rights, or encroach on their life, property, and honor. So important is this matter that Allah's Messenger, upon him be the most perfect of blessings and peace, made a point of stressing, that "the life and property of every Muslim [is] a sacred trust," in his Farewell Sermon, or that these protected. No Muslim can hurt or offend their fellow Muslim in these matters or violate their rights.

When describing the bankrupt in one of his Traditions, the Messenger of Allah, peace and blessings be upon him, presents, as it were, a vivid scene pertaining to the Hereafter: "The bankrupt of my community are those who will come on the Day of Judgment with Prayer, fasting and charity but (they will find themselves bankrupt on that day as they will have exhausted their funds of virtues) since they hurled abuse upon, brought calumny against and unlawfully consumed the wealth of others and shed the blood of others and beat others, and their virtues would be credited to the account of those (who suffered at their hand). And if their good deeds fall short to clear the account, then their sins would be recorded in (their account) and they will be thrown into Hellfire." To that end, a believer shies away from unjustly distressing their fellow believer, let alone encroaching on their sacred values such as life, property, and honor. They shudder at the prospect of having to face the repercussions of their injustice in the Hereafter.

In the continuation of the hadith under discussion it is stated that a Muslim does not surrender a fellow Muslim to the enemy. Just as a person cannot consent to having his or her own siblings handed over to the enemy and subjected to torture and punishment, a Muslim cannot accept this for their fellow believer and is obligated to approach the matter and behave in exactly the same way.

3. The hadith also states, "Allah will take care of the needs of anyone who takes care of the needs of his brother." This expression provides great incentive and inspiration to a person. In a hadith narrated by Muslim, the Messenger of Allah, peace and blessings be upon him, says, "Allah comes to the aid of His servants so long as His servants come to the aid of their fellow Muslims." This matter is presented here in such a way that it is though what is expected from the Muslim is this characteristic of being at the aid of their fellow believers becoming their second nature, so to speak. Moreover, the Prophet enjoins believers to "Help [their] brother, whether they are an oppressor or the oppressed." When it was then asked how it would be possible to help them if they are an oppressor, he replied,

"By preventing them from oppressing others." That is to say, one should not forego providing aid to others in any case.

The Prophet indicates this in the hadith, "Believers are like two hands: one washes the other."

4. The last section of the hadith proclaims that whoever screens the shortcomings and flaws of their fellow believer, Allah will screen their shortcomings and flaws on the Day of Judgment, at the most dreadful hour and terrifying place where a person is to be disgraced, and does not abase them before all humankind. What a great proposal is this! It is for this reason that Allah has not charged any of His servants with seeking out the faults of others. Moreover, in the words of a blessed servant, "Allah does not grant anyone authority to expose the faults of another." Allah is the All-Veiler, Who veils the shame, shortcomings, faults, and sins of His servants, and He commands His servants to veil both their own sins, as well as the sins of their fellow believers.

WHAT WE HAVE LEARNED

1. Allah has associated and connected fellowship to firm foundations through such vivid examples. **2.** Allah has guaranteed that the reward of such fellowship between believers will be conferred upon them, beyond measure, by Allah Himself. **3.** Mutual trust between human beings is essential for a much more livable and happy world.

UNIT NINETEEN

PRAYER

عَنْ أَبِي هُرَيْرَةَ قَالَ: سَمِعْتُ رَسُولَ اللهِ صَلَّى اللهُ عَلَيْهِ وَسَلَّمَ يَقُولُ:

"أَرَأَيْتُمْ لَوْ أَنَّ نَهْرًا بِبَابِ أَحَدِكُمْ يَغْتَسِلُ مِنْهُ كُلَّ يَوْمٍ خَمْسَ مَرَّاتٍ

هَلْ يَبْقَى مِنْ دَرَنِهِ شَيْءٌ؟" قَالُوا: لَا يَبْقَى مِنْ دَرَنِهِ شَيْءٌ، قَالَ:

فَذٰلِكَ مَثَلُ الصَّلَوَاتِ الْخَمْسِ، يَمْحُو اللهُ بِهِنَّ الْخَطَايَا.

TRANSLATION

It is related from Abu Hurayra, may Allah be pleased with him, that he heard the Messenger of Allah, may Allah bless him and grant him peace, say: "What do you think would happen if there was a river by someone's door in which he washed five times every day? Do you think that any dirt would remain on him?" They said, "Not a scrap of dirt would remain on him." He said: "That is a metaphor of the five Prayers by which Allah wipes out wrong actions." (*Sahih al-Bukhari*, Mawaqit, 6; *Sahih Muslim*, Masajid, 283. Also *see*: *Sunan at-Tirmidhi*, Amthal, 5; *Sunan an-Nasa'i*, Salah, 7; *Sunan ibn Majah*, Iqama, 193).

NARRATOR

Abu Hurayra

EXPLANATION

In this hadith, the Messenger of Allah, peace and blessings be upon him, describes the Prescribed Prayer using allegory, as this is one of the easiest and most effective means of learning and instruction. A person contemplating the similitude employed here would have no difficulty comprehending the fact that no trace of impurity would remain on a person who bathes in a river five times each day. This is because a person purifies their body and clothing of visible and palpable dirt by means of washing them with water.

With reference to this widely accepted fact, Allah's Messenger, peace and blessings be upon him, proclaims that the Prescribed Prayer cleanses a person thus, of the sins and shortcomings that signify spiritual contamination. In addition to the Prayer itself, the ritual ablution performed prior to the Prayer also provides physical cleansing. As is evident throughout the Prophetic Traditions, the ablution too is atonement for certain minor sins and misdeeds. In this way, both the ablution and the Prescribed Prayer purifies a person physically as well as spiritually. Due to the absolute nature of the statements expressed here, they are viewed as encompassing all sins, minor and major.

The terms *fahsha* (all kinds of sin) and *munkar* (every kind of evil) employed in the hadith generally signify the major sins. One who does not observe the Prescribed Prayer cannot be protected from committing the major sins, as neglecting the Prescribed Prayer is in and of itself one of the major sins. It is envisaged that a person who enters the Divine presence five times each day in full awareness of this form of worship, acts in the consciousness of forever being in Allah's presence, even outside their Prayer. Such a person does not sin knowingly; as for that which they commit unwittingly, the ablution and Prescribed Prayer serve as atonement therein.

LESSONS FROM THE HADITH

1. The Prescribed Prayer constitutes the most important and most meritorious act of daily worship incumbent upon every Muslim who has reached the age of religious responsibility (*aqil baligh*).
2. The Prayer must be observed in full awareness and consciousness of being in the Divine presence.
3. Regular and conscious observance of the five Daily Prayers protects a person from committing the major sins.
4. The Prayer is a means to Allah's forgiving the minor sins a person commits unintentionally and unconsciously.
5. Using kind counsel and words of wisdom when inviting people to goodness and when conveying to them the message of Islam, and providing examples is a mode of the Prophetic speech. We too must act in the same manner.

UNIT TWENTY

SEVEN GROUPS OF PEOPLE

عَنْ أَبِي هُرَيْرَةَ عَنِ النَّبِيِّ صَلَّى اللهُ عَلَيْهِ وَسَلَّمَ قَالَ: سَبْعَةٌ يُظِلُّهُمُ اللهُ فِي ظِلِّهِ

يَوْمَ لَا ظِلَّ إِلَّا ظِلُّهُ: إِمَامٌ عَادِلٌ، وَشَابٌّ نَشَأَ فِي عِبَادَةِ اللهِ، وَرَجُلٌ قَلْبُهُ مُعَلَّقٌ

بِالْمَسَاجِدِ وَرَجُلَانِ تَحَابَّا فِي اللهِ اجْتَمَعَا عَلَيْهِ وَتَفَرَّقَا عَلَيْهِ، وَرَجُلٌ دَعَتْهُ امْرَأَةٌ

ذَاتُ مَنْصِبٍ وَجَمَالٍ فَقَالَ إِنِّي أَخَافُ اللهَ، وَرَجُلٌ تَصَدَّقَ بِصَدَقَةٍ فَأَخْفَاهَا

حَتَّى لَا تَعْلَمَ شِمَالُهُ مَا تُنْفِقُ يَمِينُهُ، وَرَجُلٌ ذَكَرَ اللهَ خَالِيًا فَفَاضَتْ عَيْنَاهُ.

TRANSLATION

Abu Hurayra, may Allah be pleased with him, reported that the Prophet, may Allah bless him and grant him peace, said: "Allah will shade seven (groups) of people under His shade on the Day when there will be no shade except His: the just ruler; young people who have grown up in worship of Allah, may He be glorified; those people who are greatly attached to mosques; two persons who love each other for Allah's sake, meet and then leave each other because of this love; men who refuse the invitations of beautiful women of rank, saying: "I fear Allah"; those who spend in the way of Allah so secretly that when they give charity to the one on his left, the one on the right does not see it; and those whose eyes fill with tears when they mention Allah in seclusion." (*Sahih al-Bukhari*, Zakah, 16, Riqaq, 24, Hudud, 19; *Sahih Muslim*, Zakah, 91).

NARRATOR

Abu Hurayra

EXPLANATION

1. **The Just Ruler:** Justice is the principle of equity, fairness and upholding what is just, passing fair judgment, and refraining from in-

justice and favoritism and prejudice. It is declared in the verse recited at the end of every Friday sermon, "Allah enjoins justice (and right
judgment in all matters), and devotion to doing good, and generosity towards relatives, and He forbids you indecency, wickedness and
vile conduct (all offenses against religion, life, personal property,
chastity, and health of mind and body). He exhorts you (repeatedly)
so that you may reflect and be mindful!" All people are charged
with justice. Where there is justice, there is peace and goodness.
Consider a family in which a father does not adhere to the stan-
dards of justice when dealing with family members, treats them differently and does not love them equally. Can there be peace in such
a family? Can the members of that family retain their mutual love
and respect? This is not possible. That the people whom Allah will
esteem the most on the Day of Judgment are those who are just in
their dealings, has been revealed by the Prophet: "The most loved
person by Allah the Almighty on the Day of Judgment and nearest
to Him is a just ruler."

2. **Young People Who Have Grown up in Worship of Allah:** A
young person who is grows up in worship of Allah implies one who
unswervingly observes all their obligatory worship from the age of
puberty onwards, and who is preoccupied with good works and service towards their family and all humanity. The human being has
three phases throughout their life: childhood, youth, and old age. The
most important of these and that which is most instrumental in a person's life is undoubtedly their youth. For the most part, during this
phase a person is in good health. They are impressionable and resolute in the face of events. They have the strength to undertake whatever task they put their mind to and perform their worship of Allah in
great joy and happiness. Like all other bounties, the importance of
youth is known after it is lost. A poet expresses this as follows: "If but
youth could have returned and I explained to it what old age has
done to me!" However, those days have long passed and it is not

possible to bring them back. Hence, one must know the value of youth while they still possess it and must actively seek to make the best use of it. Thus, it is these people who make use of their youth well that Allah the Almighty will reward in on the Day of Judgment.

3. **Those People Who Are Greatly Attached to Mosques:** Mosques are places wherein Allah is worshipped and where the spirit attains tranquility. These places are those in which only the worship of Allah is observed. A person whose heart is attached to the mosque is one who observes their Daily Prayers in the mosque. The Prayer can, in effect, be performed everywhere; however, the reward for Prayer performed in congregation in mosques is greater by virtue of their being sites of worship exclusively. A person whose heart is attached to the mosque is a person who seeks this reward.

4. **Love for Allah's Sake:** The greatest of love is to love a person for the sake of Allah. There are many people whom we do not know, but love. Just as we do not see them, a relationship based on self-interest is not in question. We love them purely for the sake of Allah and due to the works they undertake in view of earning Allah's approval. The Companions of the noble Prophet, the first Muslims who served Islam, are among these people whom we love, despite our not being able to see them. We love them because they were the first to believe in Allah's Messenger, peace and blessings be upon him, and they patiently endured every kind of sacrifice in this cause.

5. **Fear of Allah:** A human being's carnal self seeks to do whatever it may desire, without differentiating between the shameful and prohibited, and the lawful. That which discerns good from evil is the intellect. It is through the intellect that a person refrains from the base and unlawful and desires to do what is good and beneficial. That which ensures that a rational individual distinguishes between good and evil and avoids wickedness is either the law or fear of Allah. The latter is without a doubt the most powerful of these. If a person

are able to commit an evil or injustice away from the gaze of the people and, as a result, from the gaze of the law, they will. As the people are not aware of what they have done, they go unpunished and, therefore, assume that they will get away with what they have done. A person, however, who believes in Allah, is conscious of all that they do, and knows that He will call them to account cannot perpetrate evil or injustice even when alone. The fact that those in whose hearts the fear of Allah and reverence towards Him has become firmly established will live in happiness in the world and that they will attain great rewards in the Hereafter has been announced in the Qur'an as follows:

وَاَمَّا مَنْ خَافَ مَقَامَ رَبِّهِ وَنَهَى النَّفْسَ عَنِ الْهَوٰى ۞ فَاِنَّ الْجَنَّةَ هِىَ الْمَاْوٰى

But as for him who lived in awe of his Lord, being ever conscious of His seeing him and of the standing before Him (in the Hereafter), and held back his carnal soul from lusts and caprices, surely Paradise will be his (final) refuge." (an-Nazi'at 79:40-41).

وَلِمَنْ خَافَ مَقَامَ رَبِّهِ جَنَّتَانِ

But for him who lives in awe of his Lord and of the standing before his Lord (in the Hereafter), there will be two Gardens. (ar-Rahman 55:46).

6. **Spending in the Way of Allah Secretly:** It is declared in the Qur'an:

اِنْ تُبْدُوا الصَّدَقَاتِ فَنِعِمَّا هِىَ وَاِنْ تُخْفُوهَا وَتُؤْتُوهَا الْفُقَرَاءَ فَهُوَ خَيْرٌ لَكُمْ وَيُكَفِّرُ عَنْكُمْ مِنْ سَيِّاٰتِكُمْ وَاللهُ بِمَا تَعْمَلُونَ خَبِيرٌ

> If you dispense your alms openly, it is well, but if you conceal it and give it to the poor (in secret), this is better for you; and Allah will (make it an atonement to) blot out some of your evil deeds. Allah is fully aware of all that you do. (al-Baqarah 2:271)

The verse reveals that the charity given to the poor and needy can be given publicly, but that giving in secret is better than giving openly, as alms offered in secret is free of show and preserves the self-respect of the needy. However, if giving alms openly serves the purpose of encouraging others to give in alms also, then giving in such a way is more meritorious. The Prophet said, "Giving alms secretly is more meritorious than giving them openly. For the person who wishes others to follow him, it is more meritorious to give them openly." When it comes to the prescribed annual alms, or the *zakah*, it is better to give these openly.

7. **The Eyes Filling with Tears When Mentioning Allah in Seclusion:** While Allah can be invoked at any time and place, invoking Him in seclusion is an attitude that is free of pretense. A person's eyes welling with tears in solitude is an expression of fear of Allah as well as the deep reverence felt towards Him. Allah is pleased with His servant's thus refraining from affectation. The Prophet states: "There is nothing more beloved to Allah than two drops and two marks: A tear shed due to fear of Allah, and a drop of blood shed in the path of Allah. And the two marks are the marks caused in the path of Allah, and that caused by fulfilling one of the duties made obligatory by Allah."

Thus, the Messenger of Allah, peace and blessings be upon him, announces that these seven groups of people will rise to a level on the Day of Judgment which even the Prophets will envy and that they will attain the happiness of being shaded in the shade of Allah. How happy are those who can rank among these seven groups!

WHAT WE HAVE LEARNED

1. Allah is pleased with only those deeds of His servants aimed towards His approval and takes them under His protection when there will be no other refuge.

2. The characteristics and deeds of the seven groups of people mentioned in the hadiths are of an exemplary and superior nature.

3. At the root of every good and acceptable undertaking lies a superior virtue such as loving another for the sake of Allah.

4. It is essential to keep hearts animated with love of Allah, and both love and dislike for the sake of Allah.

EVALUATION

1. What are the seven groups of people to be in the shade of the Divine Throne?

2. What is charity and what is its most acceptable form?

3. What rewards await a youth who weeps out of fear of Allah?

REFERENCES

Ahmad ibn Hanbal, *Musnad*, Beirut, 1985.

_____, *Kitabu'l-Ilal wa Ma'rifati'r-Rijal*, Talat Koçyiğit, İsmail Cerrahoğlu, İstanbul 1987.

Asım Efendi, *Kamus Tercemesi*, İstanbul, 1305/1888.

Aydınlı, Abdullah, *Hadiste Tesbit Yöntemi*, İstanbul 2003.

_____, *Hadis Istılahları Sözlüğü*, İstanbul 1987.

Ahmed Naim, *Tecrid-i Sarih Tercemesi ve Şerhi (Mukaddime)*, Ankara 1980.

Ali ibn al-Madini, *Ilalu'l-Hadith*, Abdulmu'ti Amin Kal'aci, Halab, 1980.

Aliyyulqari, *Sharhu Sharhi Nuhbati'l-Fikar*, Muhammad Nizar Tamim-Haysam Nizar Tamim, Beirut, nd.

Aşık, Nevzat, *Sahabe ve Hadis Rivayeti*, İzmir, 1981.

Aşıkkutlu, Emin, *Hadiste Rical Tenkidi*, İstanbul, 1997.

Atan, Abdullah Hikmet, "Mana ile Hadis Rivayeti," Marmara University, dissertation, İstanbul, 1999.

A'zami, Muhammad Mustafa, *İlk Devir Hadis Edebiyatı*, tr. Hulusi Yavuz, İstanbul, 1993.

Bazzar, Abu Bakr Ahmad ibn Amr, *Al-Bahru'z-Zahhar*, Mahfuzurrahman Zaynullah, Medina, 1988.

Bukhari, Muhammad ibn Ismail, *Al-Jami'u's-Sahih*, İstanbul, 1981.

_____, *At-Tarikh al-Kabir*, Haydarabad, 1943.

Çakan, İsmail Lütfi, *Hadis Usulü Şekil ve Örneklerle*, İstanbul, 1990.

_____, *Anahatlarıyla Hadis Bilgisi-Tarihi-Dindeki Yeri ve Okuma-Okutma Yöntemi*, İstanbul, 2005.

Çapan, Ergün, *Kur'an-ı Kerim'de Sahabe*, İzmir, 2002.

Darakutni, Ali ibn Umar, *Sunan*, Medina, 1966.

Abu'l-Baqa Ayyub ibn Musa, *Al-Kulliyat Mu'jam fi'l-Mustalahat wa'l-Furuqi'l-Lughawiyya*, Adnan Darwish; Muhammad al-Misri, Beirut, 1993.

Abu Dawud, Sulayman ibn al-Ash'as as-Sijistani, *Sunan*, Beirut, 1988.

Abu Gudda, Abdulfattah, *Al-Isnad mina'd-Din*, Halab, 1992.

Abu Ya'la al-Mawsali, *Musnad*, Husayn Salim Asad, Beirut, 1986.

Abu Zur'a ar-Razi, *Kitabu'd-Du'afa*, (in *Abu Zur'a ar-Razi wa Juhuduhu fi's-Sunneti'n-Nabawiyya*), Medina, 1989.

Hakim an-Nisaburi, *Ma'rifatu Ulumi'l-Hadith*, Medina, 1977.

Halil ibn Ahmad al-Halili, *Al-Irshad fi Ma'rifati Ulamai'l-Hadith*, Beirut, 1993.

Hatib al-Baghdadi, *Al-Jami' li Ahlaqi'r-Rawi wa Adabi's-Sami*, Mahmud Tahhan, Riyad, 1983.

_____, *Al-Kifaya fi Ilmi'r-Riwaya*, Ahmed Ömer Haşim, Beirut 1986.

_____, *Ar-Rihla fi Talabi'l-Hadith*, Nurettin Itr, Beirut, 1975.

_____, *Sharafu Ashabi'l-Hadith*, M. Said Hatiboğlu, Ankara, 1991.

_____, *Tarikhu Baghdad*, Mustafa Abdulqadir Ata, Beirut 1997.

Haysami, Nuraddin Ali ibn Abi Bakr, *Majma'u'z-Zawaid wa Manba'u'l-Fawaid*, Beirut, 1982.

Humaydi, *Al-Musnad*, Habiburrahman al-A'zami, Beirut, nd.

Firuzabadi, Majduddin Muhammad ibn Ya'kub, *Al-Qamusu'l-Muhit*, Beirut, 1987.

Gülen, Fethullah, *Sonsuz Nur*, İstanbul, 1994.

Ibn Abdilbarr, Abu Umar Yusuf, *Jami'u Bayani'l-Ilm wa Fadlih,* Beirut, 1978.

_____, *At-Tamhid lima fi'l-Muwattai mina'l-Ma'ani wa'l-Asanid*, Maghrib, 1988.

Ibn Adi, Abu Ahmad Abdullah, *Al-Kamil fi Du'afai'r-Rijal*, Beirut, 1988.

Ibnu'l-Jawzi, Abu'l-Faraj Abdu'r-Rahman ibn Ali, *Al-Mawdu'at*, Beirut, 1995.

Ibn Abi Hatim, *Kitabu'l-Jarh wa't-Ta'dil*, Haydarabad, 1952, Beirut, nd.

_____, *Ilalu'l-Hadith*, Beirut, 1985.

Ibnu'l-Athir, Izzuddin Ali ibn Muhammad, *Al-Lubab fi Tahdibi'l-Ansab*, Beirut, 1980.

Ibn Hajar al-Askalani, *Lisanu'l-Mizan*, Beirut, 1987.

_____, *Tahzibu't-Tahzib*, Haydarabad, 1325, Beirut, 1968.

Ibn Hibban, *Kitabu'l-Majruhin mina'l-Muhaddisin wa'd-Du'afai wa'l-Matrukin*, Halab, 1976.

Ibn Majah, Abu Abdillah Muhammad ibn Yazid al-Qazwini, *Sunan*, Muhammad Fuad Abdulbaqi, Beirut, 1975.

Ibn Manzur, *Lisanu'l-Arab*, Beirut, nd.

Ibn Rajab al-Hanbali, *Sharhu Ilali't-Tirmidhi,* Hammam Abdu'r-Rahim Said, Jordan, 1987.

Ibn Sa'd, *At-Tabaqatu'l-Kubra*, Muhammad Abdulqadir Ata, Beirut, 1990.

Ibnu's-Salah ash-Shahrizuri, *Ulumu'l-Hadith*, Nuraddin Itr, Damascus, 1986.

Imtiyaz, Ahmad, *Dalailu't-Tawthiqi'l-Mubakkir li's-Sunnati wa'l-Hadith*, Cairo, 1990.

Qadi Iyaz, *Al-Ilma ila Ma'rifati Usuli'r-Riwaya wa Taqyidi's-Sama*, Sayyid Ahmad Sakr, Cairo, nd.

Koçyiğit, Talat, *Hadis Tarihi*, Ankara, 1981.

Malik ibn Anas, *Muwatta*, Muhammad Fuad Abdulbaqi, Cairo, nd.

Muslim, Abu'l-Husayn Muslim ibn Hajjaj al-Kushayri, *Sahih Muslim*, Muhammad ibn Nizar Tamim-Haysam ibn Nizar Tamim, Beirut, 1999.

Nasa'i, Ahmad ibn Ali, *Sunan*, Beirut, nd.

_____, *As-Sunanu'l-Kubra*, Beirut, 1991.

Ramahurmuzi, Hasan ibn Abdu'r-Rahman, *Al-Muhaddisu'l-Fasil bayna'r-Rawi wa'l-Wai*, Muhammad Ajjaj al-Hatib, Beirut, 1984.

Rif'at Fawzi Abdilmuttalib, *Tawthiq as-Sunna fi'l-Qarn al-Thani al-Hijri,* Cairo, 1981.

Sa'di al-Hashimi, *Abu Zur'a ar-Razi wa Juhuduhu fi's-Sunnati'n-Nabawiyya*, Medina, 1989.

Said ibn Mansur, *Sunan*, Sa'd b. Abdullah, Riyad, 1993.

Sahawi, Shamsuddin Muhammad ibn Abdu'r-Rahman, *Fathu'l-Mughis Sharhu Alfiyati'l-Hadith*, Ali Husayn Ali, Cairo, 1995.

Sam'ani, Abu Sa'd Abdulkarim ibn Muhammad, *Al-Ansab*, Beirut, 1981.

Sezgin, Fuad, *Buhari'nin Kaynakları,* İstanbul, 1956.

_____, "Rivayet Literatürünün Gelişimi," in *Buhari'nin Kaynakları*, Ankara, 2000.

Subhi Salih, *Hadis İlimleri ve Hadis Istılahları*, tr. M. Yaşar Kandemir, Ankara, 1981.

Tabarani, Sulayman ibn Ahmad, *Al-Mu'jamu'l-Kabir*, Hamdi Abdulmajid as-Salafi, Baghdad, 1978.

_____, *Al-Mu'jamu'l-Awsat*, Muhammad Hasan Muhammad, Beirut, 1999.

Tahawi, Abu Ja'far, *Sharhu Mushkili'l-Athar,* Shuayb al-Arnaut, Beirut, 1994.

Tirmidhi, Abu Isa Muhammad ibn Isa, *Al-Jami'u's-Sahih,* Ahmad Muhammad Shakir, Beirut, nd.

Yahya ibn Ma'in, *Tarikh Riwayatu Abbas ibn Muhammad ad-Duri*, Ahmad Muhammad Nur Sayf, Mecca, 1979.

Yardım, Ali, *Hadis I-II*, İstanbul, 2000.

Yücel, Ahmed, *Hadis Istılahlarının Doğuşu ve Gelişimi*, İstanbul, 1996.

Zahabi, Shamsuddin Muhammad ibn Ahmad, *Mizanu'l-Itidal fi Nakdi'r-Rijal,* Ali Muhammad Mu'awwiz-Adil Ahmad Abdulmawjud, Beirut, 1995.

_____, *Siyaru A'lami'n-Nubala*, Shu'ayb al-Arnaut, Beirut, 1993.

_____, *Tadhkiratu'l-Huffaz*, Haydarabad, 1956, Beirut, nd.